CHURCHILL AND THE KING

CHURCHILL
AND THE KING

THE WARTIME ALLIANCE OF
Winston Churchill AND George VI

Kenneth
Weisbrode

VIKING

VIKING
Published by the Penguin Group
Penguin Group (USA) LLC
375 Hudson Street
New York, New York 10014

USA | Canada | UK | Ireland | Australia | New Zealand | India | South Africa | China
penguin.com
A Penguin Random House Company

First published by Viking Penguin, a member of Penguin Group (USA) LLC, 2013

Library of Congress Cataloging-in-Publication Data

Weisbrode, Kenneth.
Churchill and the king : the wartime alliance of Winston Churchill and George VI /
Kenneth Weisbrode.
pages cm
Includes bibliographical references and index.
ISBN 978-0-670-02576-3
1. Churchill, Winston, 1874–1965—Friends and associates. 2. George VI, King of Great
Britain, 1895–1952—Friends and associates. 3. World War, 1939–1945—Great
Britain. 4. Great Britain—History—George VI, 1936-1952 I. Title.
DA587.W45 2013
941.083092'2—dc23
[B]   2013017201

Printed in the United States of America
10 9 8 7 6 5 4 3 2 1

Set in Warnock Pro with Boberia Com
Designed by Daniel Lagin

For my mother, my sister, and my late father

CONTENTS

CONTENTS

PREFACE

"Your Majesty's treatment of me has been intimate and generous to a degree that I had never deemed possible." So wrote Winston Churchill to King George VI in January 1941, just after Britain had endured its darkest hour. There was more to the statement than courtesy. Some people have said that only Churchill could have saved the country at that moment. They have also said that if he had failed, the king would almost certainly have lost his throne and probably much more. The statements may be qualified in various ways, but most amount to the same thing: Winston Churchill was the necessary man. Though it has been a debatable point, few have said it about George VI. But no one who knows the king's war record would call him an idle spectator. A verdict does not issue easily for either man on his own. The real question is: Where would each man have been without the other?

Viewers of the 2010 film *The King's Speech* came away with a new appreciation of the trials and triumphs of the unexpected king; those in the know detected its odd and inaccurate portrayal of

Churchill. He was, as he probably had to be to some extent, the Churchill of caricature, with cigar, grimace, and growl. But to have shown him strongly in favor of abdication did a disservice. So did the superficial, even supercilious, way he appeared to treat the new king. Did it really happen this way? Was that all? What about the war?

The story of what happened between these men tells us something important about the position and purpose of the British monarchy, then and now. It has been an effective institution for binding the nation (and back then, the empire) together; if not, it would have disappeared long ago. But is it still necessary? That so many people in Britain and elsewhere continue to revere it must come down to more than tradition, sentimentality, and personal affection for a few particular members of the royal family. There must be, in other words, a better reason for its survival.

Rulership, like leadership, is a puzzle. It is not just an assemblage of policy, personality, intelligence, charisma, and power but of some changeable and often unpredictable chemistry among all these elements and also between the ruler and the ruled. It may be true that the best things in life are done in combination. Success is almost never solitary. Yet why some rulers succeed while others fail may be impossible to understand. The British case is complicated further by the existence of an unwritten constitution, enforced by custom, habit, and instinct. This book addresses the puzzle by exploring the alliance of a British king and prime minister during a most difficult time. George VI became king after the abdication of his brother in 1936. Winston Churchill became prime minister after the fall of Neville Chamberlain four years later. Britain and its empire would soon fight alone against a resurgent Germany. The two men met nearly every week whenever both were in London. Each was, in his own way, admired, even beloved, by many of his countrymen. Theirs was an alliance that came to be one of trust and fellowship, even friendship, but it was none of these things initially, nor was it simply an association of convenience. It was one of several partnerships that each man made that mattered. Partnerships are often limited. They can be dissolved. Alliances take things a step further. Genuine alliances are indivisible. In deriving its strength from the life mettle of both men, this alliance set an example and a precedent that would outlive them both.

Why did this alliance work so well? Was it the product of crisis? Or were the two men predestined for mutual sympathy? Upon what was such sympathy based? Churchill had come to power after a long and complicated political career; many people mistrusted him. He was an embattled man facing a losing war. The king came up unprepared, unconfident, and perhaps unwilling to rule. On the face of it, the two would appear to have inspired little hope, but history suggests otherwise. Churchill could not have been the leader he was without having had so strong a working relationship with his monarch. The king—and more to the point, the monarchy and the British nation—could not have endured the war without it.

These points may have more to do with the essence of modern leadership than with its exercise by this monarchy or any single leader. It has been said that today's world is leaderless. The observation tends to conflate what leadership is with what it does. How do leaders earn trust? How do they collaborate with rivals? How do they come to know themselves—their strengths, weaknesses, and vulnerabilities? How do they manage to find what they most need from others without appearing weak and flawed? If they succeed, is a fall from popular grace inevitable? Even the Churchills of this world have limited and diminishing capacity to rule. Power usually falls after it rises. In the race to preserve it, how do they make use of allies, adversaries, interests, habits, perceptions, and expectations while maintaining or furthering their own unique, innate character, which, in most cases, compelled their urge to lead in the first place? And how do they go on to mold, meld, and adapt that character with that of others, and to augment it?

Students of history learn something when they set out to understand the past: that it is never complete; it is a perpetual argument, or what Churchill called "a scenario without an end," filled with puzzles and gaps. Because it is impossible to re-create the past entirely—there are no time machines—new attempts, no matter how exhaustive or repetitious, will always raise new questions and complicate the ones that have been asked and answered. And they will always contain holes.

The world does not need another hagiography of Churchill or the royal family, and this book will be that for neither. "We have been told more about Winston Churchill than any other human being," Max Hastings has written, with some license. "Yet much remains opaque, because he wished it thus." The king's official biographer, John Wheeler-Bennett, posed it in the form of a question about Churchill over forty years ago: "Has not every aspect of his Protean career been covered—and amply—either by himself or by others?" A generation hence, the answer to Wheeler-Bennett's question may well be no. After poring over the same anecdotes, aphorisms, speeches, and quarrels over who said what exactly and why, it appears that so obvious and apparent a relationship—that between the prime minister and his king—has been taken for granted, with studies by David Cannadine, Philip Ziegler, and Robert Rhodes James being among the very few perceptive exceptions.

It may seem strange or unwise for an American who has never been enamored of British royalty, or of Winston Churchill, for that matter, to revisit them. Both paths have been well trod, to put it mildly. But once I began to think about them, I was struck by the gap hiding in plain sight: Why has so little been written about what went on between these two important figures, and how did that affect history?

This relationship was important. Both men were champions against adversity. Each had lived with it his entire life. Both nearly died from it. It brought them together as much as any other factor, person, or event, and it merits recognition in its full spectrum or as that favorite British formulation—the concentric circle—might depict it. A concentric circle of adversity would place Churchill and the king as moving back and forth through the rings of family, upbringing, career, character, and the war, all presenting obstacles, challenges, and affirmations of their deepening partnership as it evolved, both in time and in reference to their separate pasts, as well as to their future legacies. The various roles they played to and for each other—foil, confidant, fellow traveler, conspirator, and comrade—blur so that the full effect, again, was exponential. The story of such an alliance will by necessity tread over familiar ground to many readers, but the aficionados among them will, I hope, see old facts in a new light.

This book is written for anyone who has wondered why some leaders and nations succeed against great odds. The varieties of allied success are infinite as well as important. Like biographies of Winston Churchill and the British royal family, their mysteries will remain with us for a long time to come.

CHURCHILL AND THE KING

CHAPTER ONE
Churchill's Moment

Neville Chamberlain had taken far too long, some said, to admit failure. So they gave him a hard push. Britain's prime minister imagined that he had appeased Hitler. He may have deterred him, but only for a brief time. He did not dissuade, disarm, or destroy him. Hitler took the Sudetenland and dismembered Czechoslovakia; he had conquered his piece of Poland and allowed Stalin to grab the rest; he had invaded Denmark and Norway, "fascinated, browbeaten, cajoled and then garotted." The way was open to France, and everyone, or nearly everyone, knew it. In May 1940, Europe was again at war. And in Britain, Chamberlain got the blame.

The king was worried. He had seen his father age terribly during the last war and had served in it himself. He may have had "boundless confidence" in his prime minister, but Chamberlain had failed. "Resign—Resign," the members of Parliament shouted amid stanzas of "Rule Britannia." The burden of choosing a successor fell to them and, ultimately, to the British people. But the formal responsibility rested with the king, for the king is the only one who can ask a prime minister to form a government.

The most likely candidate to replace him was Lord Halifax, the foreign secretary. "The Holy Fox," as Churchill had named him, was a tall, trim, elegant Yorkshireman and a former viceroy of India, whose "long figure curled like a question mark." He was at once skeptical and imaginative—a man, it was said, who "could see at least three more facets to any diamond than the jewelers who cut it had placed there." One of the few sympathetic qualities of this "high priest of the Respectable Tendency," perhaps, was his possession, like the king, of a speech impediment that was said to resemble "a slight lisp." He was also missing a hand.

Halifax was a man after the king's heart: aristocratic in style and spirit, resilient, stately, shrewd, cautious, principled, practical, courteous, attentive, and, probably above all else, "insinuating, but unlovable." He was, therefore, a reliable figure, not at all like the unpredictable Churchill, whom Chamberlain regarded as a "d——d uncomfortable bed fellow." The king trusted Halifax and was said to be "far closer to him than to any other senior politician of the day." His wife was a lady-in-waiting to the queen, and it had been he who had convinced the king, ultimately, that the policy of appeasement had been misguided.

But Halifax did not want the job and made a strong case for why he should not have it. He was already a member of the House of Lords; prime ministers generally came from the Commons. As foreign secretary he was associated in the popular mind with Chamberlain, whereas Churchill, though he had been serving until now as First Lord of the Admiralty, had been the prime minister's loudest critic. Halifax suggested a government of national unity with members of each major party, but not with himself as head. According to him, Chamberlain

> thought that it was clearly Winston, or myself, and appeared to suggest that if it were myself he might continue to serve in the Government. I put all the arguments that I could think of against myself, laying a considerable emphasis on the difficult position of a Prime Minister unable to make contact with the centre of gravity in the House of Commons. The P.M. did not think so much of this . . . and my stomach ache continued. I then said . . . that I had no doubt at all in my own mind that for me to take it would create a quite impossible position.

Therefore,

> it would be hopeless. . . . If I was not in charge of the war (operations) and if I didn't lead in the House, I should be a cypher. I thought Winston was a better choice.

A new government would also need the support of the leaders of the Labour Party, which either man probably could have got, but not under Chamberlain.

The three met together at Downing Street. Chamberlain's "demeanour was cool, unruffled and seemingly quite detached from the personal aspect of the affair."

"Can you see any reason, Winston, why in these days a Peer should not be Prime Minister?"

Churchill "saw a trap in this question." His friend and fixer, Brendan Bracken, had warned him the previous night to expect it.

"It would be difficult to say yes without saying frankly that he thought he himself should be the choice. If he said no, or hedged, he felt sure that Mr. Chamberlain would turn to Lord Halifax and say, 'Well, since Winston agrees I am sure that if the King asks me I should suggest his sending for you.'" Churchill said that Chamberlain probably wanted him to serve as Halifax's deputy and he was open to the possibility. "You cannot agree to this," Bracken said.

"Winston was obdurate; he said that he could not go back on his word." So Bracken told him to keep quiet.

"Promise?"

He did.

Churchill stared out the window and said nothing. "I have had many important interviews in my public life and this was certainly the most important," he later wrote. "Usually I talk a great deal, but on this occasion I was silent. . . . As I remained silent, a very long pause ensued." Halifax proposed that Chamberlain should nominate Churchill to succeed him. Churchill finally spoke and said he would take no political steps until he heard from the king. His son, Randolph, later modified the story:

It was quite true that Winston had been advised to keep quiet when he went with Halifax to see Chamberlain. It was also true that Chamberlain wanted Halifax and said that Halifax would be more acceptable to Labour and to the Liberals. It was also true that Halifax had said that he would not be captain of his own ship with Winston on board. W.S.C. had then spoken and said: "I am sure you wouldn't." Chamberlain had then suggested further discussion with the Labour Party. Winston had replied that he would have nothing to do with further discussions. If the King sent for him, he would form a government whether Labour came in or not.

Thus did Churchill emerge as the new leader.

The king had been feeling unhappy. His thoughts were said to be charitable, even sympathetic, toward Chamberlain, and he regretted the attacks on him. He was worried about the Labour Party leaders. He asked, "Would they serve in the Nat. Govt. with N. Chamberlain as P.M.? They said no. Would they serve in the Nat. Govt. with anybody else as P.M.?"

For his part, Churchill did "not remember exactly how things happened" but that he became aware that "I might well be called upon to take the lead." He remembered being "content to let events unfold. . . . It was a bright, sunny afternoon, and Lord Halifax and I sat for a while on a seat in the garden of Number 10 and talked about nothing in particular."

On the next day, May 10, the news came that Hitler's armies had invaded Holland and Belgium. Churchill treated himself to a 4:00 a.m. breakfast of fried eggs and bacon, and a cigar. Later he discussed with the War Cabinet the effect of the previous night's attacks. Halifax had gone to the dentist. Chamberlain then went to the palace. The king

accepted his resignation, & told him how grossly unfai[r] I thought he had been treated, & that I was terribly sorry that all this controversy had happened. We then had an informal talk over his successor. I, of course, suggested Halifax, but he told me that H. was not enthusiastic, as being in the Lords he could only act as a shadow o[r] a ghost in the Commons. I was disappointed over this statement, as I thought H. was the obvious man, & that his peerage could be placed in abeyance for the time being. Then I knew that there was only one person I could send for to form a Government who had the confidence of the country, & that was Winston. I asked Chamberlain his advice, & he told me Winston was the man to send for.

So he did. When Churchill arrived at the palace that evening, he

was taken immediately to the King. His Majesty received me most graciously and bade me sit down. He looked at me searchingly and quizzically for some moments, and then said: "I suppose you don't know why I have sent for you?" Adopting his mood, I replied: "Sir, I simply couldn't imagine why." He laughed and said: "I want to ask you to form a Government." I said I would certainly do so.

Churchill rode from the palace "in complete silence." Arriving back at the Admiralty, he remarked to his detective, W. H. Thompson:

"You know why I have been to Buckingham Palace, Thompson?"

"Yes, sir . . ." Thompson saw tears.

"God alone knows how great it is," Churchill said. "I hope that it is not too late. I am very much afraid that it is. We can only do our best." Then he "muttered something to himself" and strode up the stairs, "with a look of determination, mastering all emotion."

It has been said that insouciance is the elixir of power. It is difficult to imagine Churchill or the king drinking in excess from that cup. Neither man was all-powerful politically: one was head of government, the other head of state. Neither was a Roosevelt nor a Stalin. But "[t]ogether"—to borrow a description once applied to Churchill and his amanuensis, Eddie Marsh—"this strangely assorted pair, the bulldog and the sparrow, plunged into the turmoil of politics without a moment's delay."

The question remains whether the extroverted and introverted elements of their character were inherently complementary; that is, whether each man strove consciously to work with the other so as to make an amalgam. They certainly warmed to each other. But the prospect of an alliance was not self-evident, at least not initially. It was fortunate that getting on, even developing a mutual affection, may have proved less difficult than either man had imagined, if they had even thought about it so directly. Somehow they made it work.

Halifax had been magnificently right. For Halifax was insouciant, in or out of power. He was practically a member of the king's family; the two spoke each other's language and had dealt familiarly for a long time. Halifax would have had no trouble working with him. Chamberlain's rationale for not having recommended him to the king remains unresolved. He had said to Halifax "that he had always thought he [Chamberlain] could not face the job of being prime minister in war, but when it came he did; and yet now that the war was becoming intense he could not but feel relieved that the final responsibility was off him." Perhaps he thought he was doing Halifax a favor. Halifax in turn must not have felt the need to place so much importance on reordering his mind and his relations for that purpose, as Churchill later did. Familiarity and trust were already in place. Churchill, on the other hand, had to earn them.

Churchill had been the most stalwart, most eloquent, and most determined opponent of the policy of appeasement. He had a checkered political past and an even more checkered reputation for a life once described "as a set-piece contest between curriculum vitae and genius." He had served and abandoned both major political parties and had seen his career rise and fall repeatedly for nearly half a century. He had held every major cabinet post bar that of foreign secretary and prime minister, and not by accident. Some of his contemporaries abhorred the idea of his assuming office, but to his and his country's credit, Halifax recognized that Churchill, not he, was the man it needed. Only Churchill could have formed a national government to rally the nation in war. Only he could have waged it.

So he did. But he did not lead on his own; no leader does. There is an easy tendency to promote the identity of Winston Churchill as a solitary bulwark: as Britain stood alone in the darkest hours of 1940, so did Churchill. But at his side were his aides and lieutenants, his so-called Secret Circle of favorites, his parliamentary allies, and his loyal wife and family. Most of these people, however, were followers or courtiers. There was only one other man who stood with Churchill at the helm, from the very beginning, and he was the king. "Ministers come and go, but the King remains, always at the centre of public affairs, always participating vigilantly in the work of government from a standpoint detached from any consideration but the welfare of his peoples as a whole," an editorial in the *Times* put it in May 1943 after the victories in North Africa. "He is the continuous element in the constitution, one of the main safe-guards of its democratic character, and the repository of a knowledge of affairs that before long comes to transcend that of any individual statesman."

But the war caught the king unready and, apparently, unproven. In the spring of 1940, few could have predicted the calamity that was about to befall Britain. Even Churchill, for all that he had warned of it, could not have known the extent of the defeat and destruction that would come in the next few months.

"In times of danger," wrote a contemporary observer, "democratic leadership is gained, not by the gun and rubber truncheon, but by great ability, the reputation for courage in vicissitude, stamina, and fighting spirit." Churchill reached the pinnacle of British politics at last. Would another, younger prime minister have been better for the forty-five-year-old king? That was certainly possible. Would a different monarch have made Churchill's life comparably worse, pushing him harder to justify and explain every strategic decision, or, alternatively, much easier, by letting him do his job without interference? Also quite possible. "George VI was not a born leader," his father's biographer, Kenneth Rose, has written. "He could seem shy and harassed, aloof and even morose. Yet when put to the test of war he displayed nobler qualities: resolution and dignity and the chivalry of an earlier age." He, too, gained.

It is not easy to imagine either of the Edwards, VII or VIII, George V, or even Queen Victoria, for that matter—despite the interest she took in some matters of government—being granted so much direct involvement, and with no objection. This monarch had it, thanks to Churchill. The two were the better for it. So was Britain.

Who were they? Before anything can be understood of their individual or combined nature, something more must be said about their origins.

CHAPTER TWO
Uncommon Births

December 14, 1895, the day the future King George VI was born, was "Mausoleum Day." On that day in 1861 Prince Albert, the beloved and influential husband and lodestar to Queen Victoria, had died. Princess Alice, his daughter, had died on the same day in 1878. Although not quite Friday the thirteenth, "[i]t was not a tactful day" to be born.

Nor was it an easy family to enter. Great-grandmother Victoria and her descendants were an especially large and complicated brood. "Gangan" was more divine than human. Her son, later Edward VII, on the other hand, was as warm and jolly and affectionate as a grandfather could be, and his wife, Princess Alexandra, doted on her grandchildren. But the family was not a warm one. Its customs, even for royalty, were formal, augmented by the queen's habit of speaking to her relatives in German. To have been born "on a note of apology" was, somehow, appropriate.

Twenty-one years earlier at Blenheim Palace occurred another, not particularly propitious, birth. Winston, the firstborn son of Lord

Randolph Churchill and his American-born wife, Jennie, arrived several months premature and was ill from the start. The Churchills were not royalty, nor even at the top of the aristocracy. It has been said that their family motto—"Faithful but unfortunate"—was well deserved, for "all Churchills were undoubtedly eccentric even when brilliant," but they were brilliant, even dazzling, nonetheless. The family—especially the Spencer branch, from which Winston came— was far older in the English sense than the royal family. It included a few notable ancestors, such as the first Duke of Marlborough, the greatest English military figure of his—or perhaps any—time. Some may have seen this as an asset. It may not have been, because several descendants, particularly Winston, could escape neither the comparison nor the tribal solipsism that accompanied it.

His mixed parentage gave him the name the "Yankee Marlborough," and, less flatteringly, the "Yankee mongrel." The combination was said to have induced both his entrepreneurial and entitled tendencies: a status-conscious risk taker who acknowledged few inherent limits to what he could do and be. At the same time there was in him a certain indestructible quality that connected the past to the future. So mixed and conflictive a background need not assure such a life (Winston's younger brother, John, for example, was dull and conventional), but for Winston it was seen, not least by himself, to confer one of predestined chaos, or at least drama.

His mother was the daughter of the New York financier Leonard Jerome, a flamboyant, almost fantastical figure of the Gilded Age. She was one of the most beautiful women of her generation, and was, reputedly, not averse to sharing the affections of admirers. Her eldest son adored her. They were not especially close during his childhood, but they developed a partnership in which she would serve as agent, matchmaker, and promoter of his career from behind the scenes. He never ceased being grateful to—yet also, at some level, dismissive of—the exquisite lady who was his mother.

That ambivalence could have described Winston Churchill's lifelong attitude to women. He rarely spoke of them in public and seemed uninterested in them, generally preferring the company of men. When Nancy Astor walked into the House of Commons, for example, he said that he "felt as though some woman had entered my bath and I had nothing to protect myself with except my sponge." He tended to see them in black and white: as either "virginal snowdrops" or worldly-wise figures who could be of use to him. To an extent this was characteristic of the times, but in Churchill it had less to do with any moral or cultural set of norms than with his own preferences and prejudices. He was never prudish or censorious for its own sake.

Queen Mary, the wife of George V, was remote, sometimes stern, and also German. She had been her husband's late brother's fiancée. She would outlive her husband and two of her sons, keeping up her bejeweled presence until 1953. We know comparatively little about the future king's relationship with her; their letters reveal a formal affection, and he may have considered her a confidante. But it is hard to imagine them as being warm, especially given the appeal of his elder brother, known then as David—a sunny, lively, and outgoing boy, whose birth eighteen months before his own happened during Ascot week and was accompanied by festivals.

Later generations may have said it was more than slightly ironic for the British nation to be led by a prince of a German dynasty and his part-German wife, but that is how royalty is and always has been: international, or rather multinational, and complicated in ways that aren't always politically expedient. The Windsors were of recent vintage. They acquired that name during the previous war when Baron Stamfordham, the private secretary to King George V, suggested it in lieu of Saxe-Coburg and Gotha, which had an inconvenient ring to it when their country was at war with Germany. The future king's own name came from his grandfather and great-grandfather (Albert), as well as from his great-uncle, the German emperor (Frederick), another great-uncle, the Duke of Connaught (Arthur), and finally, his father (George). Most people called him Bertie.

The challenges he inherited were several generations in the making. His grandfather King Edward VII, also called Bertie, was, by the end of his short reign, well liked, even loved, as the "Uncle of Europe." His father, by contrast, was short, slight, and somber.

He is not loved, he is not feared,
The man with the receding beard.

Edward VII and Queen Alexandra led an open, vibrant, exuberant life. Their world at Marlborough House and Sandringham resembled a happy European salon. Theirs was the splendor of the Edwardian era.

Its Georgian successor could not, nor did it seem to want to, compare. George V and Queen Mary kept to a small circle. The king was not an especially complex man, nor was he especially caring, reserving his limited expressions of affection for Charlotte, his pet parrot. He could be cold, distant, and even hostile, except occasionally in written correspondence. He was overconsistent and overzealous in matters of routine and appearance, and seemed to live on the cusp of a very different age. He was dutiful and proper, but he rarely displayed enthusiasm for his role, once exclaiming, "But it's horrible! I'm not educated for the job—in fact, I'm not educated at all!!"

People eventually warmed to him because of his efforts to boost morale during the First World War, which nearly destroyed his health, and his introduction of regular broadcasts by the new technology of radio, which proved surprisingly popular. It may have made him more human and less distant. Whether this was true or not, it certainly set a precedent for the popular media monarchy. In this way the war made him. He was, if only by default, a reassuring if less than inspiring royal figure, and not merely the abusive, domineering father of the occasional caricature. Yet his relations with his children, notably with his two eldest sons, were poor. Toward them he could be an uncompromising, rigid, petty tyrant.

It is not difficult, then, to imagine Bertie regarding his father with fear, nervousness, and annoyance. For all that there was a special affinity between them, as some of their correspondence suggests, it was neither intellectual nor sufficient to compensate for the king's determination to rectify the boy's physical debilities by force. Therefore, despite the affections bestowed on Bertie by his extended family and his own great affection for Balmoral—honed by visits to his beloved and indulgent grandparents—and for Sandringham, his early life was bleak. He wore painful braces on his legs to counteract knock-knees, and was persecuted because of left-handedness and his stammer—which only became worse as a result. It was no wonder he lacked, or appeared to lack, confidence, especially as contrasted with his uninhibited and more talented elder brother. He was prone, mainly in the presence of his great-grandmother, to burst out crying, a tendency exacerbated by terrible, even sadistic, nannies until the arrival of the one he adored most, called Lalla. What he lacked in confidence he made up for with exertion, intensity, and rectitude.

Churchill also was fond of his nurse, Mrs. Everest. Theirs was his closest relationship for the first few years of his life. That was in keeping with the Victorian and Edwardian practice of child-rearing, typical of the "Nanny-archy" of the day. She alone doted upon the "pale little ghost" and became, in addition to his sole source of intimacy and constant sympathy, his principal "audience. . . . in the centre of a stage of his own creation," which included elaborate reenactments of military battles in his playroom.

He grew up into a difficult boy, not as bad-tempered as Bertie but about as querulous, ill behaved, and mischievous as a child could be. Discipline was usually absent or arbitrary. Later, at Harrow, he was often threatened with caning—neither the threat nor the action, so far as history records, impressed him—and with other punishments, such as being forced to run for hours at a time.

Churchill's feelings about Harrow were almost surely painful and hostile. His five years there, he later said, were the worst period of his life. The scar took a very long time to heal. When he visited Harrow in his thirties, he was booed by the pupils and reacted badly, especially for a politician by now accustomed to the treatment. The only change seemed to have occurred during the Second World War, for then, when he visited the school, he took part eagerly in the singing of school songs and in cheers against Hitler.

At Harrow there was an infamous incident soon after his arrival that reflected on Churchill's filial disposition. Leo Amery, later to become a political ally, was pushed into the pool from behind by Churchill, then a "rather inky small boy, grubby and obstinate." Upon learning that Amery was head of his house and in the sixth form, young Winston pointed out how easy it had been to mistake him for a nonentity given his small size. "He did not seem at all placated by this; so I added in a most brilliant recovery, 'My father, who is a great man, is also small.'"

Winston idolized his father and wished he could relate to him, somehow, as an equal. Yet even at a relatively early age he was made aware of some flaw or irony to heed in a father who may not have been "as wise as he was shrewd." He told Winston, "Do remember things do not always go right with me. My every action is misjudged and every word distorted. . . . So make some allowances." His son was just twenty-one when Lord Randolph died. He devoted the rest of his life, he said, to proving himself worthy of the father whose own political ambition had been cut short.

Winston's relationship with his father may have been even more literally distant than Bertie's with his; yet the senior Churchill remained his lodestar for some time. He memorized his speeches, wrote his biography, and adopted his political philosophy. He made the promotion of the Churchill name his life's work. It was no coincidence that the two other biographical subjects he chose, in addition to his father, were the Duke of Marlborough and himself, fictionalized as "Savrola."

"When I hear a man say that his childhood was the happiest time of his life, I think, 'my friend, you have had a pretty poor life.'" We cannot know if Churchill really believed this, but the king probably did, for there is little evidence to the contrary. "The House of Hanover, like ducks, produce bad parents—they trample on their young." Nor did their successors prepare theirs well for adulthood.

Bertie grew up surrounded by a retinue but with few actual friends or companions his own age besides his elder brother. He tended to lack sociability and was often ill at ease, which limited the possibility of building a circle of supporters. He was not only uncomfortable in society but also moody. Worst of all was his temper, lost in terrible eruptions the family called "gnashes" or "Nashvilles." The tantrums did not cease; in fact, they became worse with age. At some point in these early years he began to stammer. He was also prone to daydreaming, hyperactivity, and depression, even despair, when he failed to accomplish what he wanted. He became known as a "bad starter" but, once his determination kicked in, a keen finisher.

Bertie had been badly educated in most subjects. He knew very little about literature, philosophy, or history. His principal tutor, a Mr. Hansell, found him hopeless. His brother David was not much better. Years later, the latter returned from a weekend and exclaimed, "Look at this extraordinary little book which Lady Desborough says I ought to read. Have you ever heard of it?" It was *Jane Eyre*.

Violet Bonham Carter has told a similar story about Churchill. During their conversation at a dinner party, he told her—in what became one of his more famous epithets:

> "We are all worms. But I do believe that I am a glow-worm."
>
> By this time I was convinced of it—and my conviction remained unshaken throughout the years that followed.
>
> Later on he asked me whether I thought that words had a magic and a music quite independent of their meaning. I said

I certainly thought so, and I quoted as a classic though familiar instance the first lines that came into my head:

> *Charm'd magic casements, opening on the foam*
> *Of perilous seas, in faery lands forlorn.*

His eyes blazed with excitement. "Say that again," he said, "say it again—it is marvellous!"

"But," I objected, "you know these lines. You know the 'Ode to the [*sic*] Nightingale.'"

He had apparently never read it and never heard of it before. (I must however add that next time I met him he had learnt not merely this, but all the odes of Keats by heart—and he recited them quite mercilessly from start to finish, not sparing me a syllable.)

As a child, Winston hated memorization—at least forced memorization—disliked classical learning, and relished only games and exposure to the pageant of English history. He was otherwise a terrible student who left Harrow with little to show for the time he had spent there, apart from some useful education in the English language: his compensation for having been unable to succeed with Greek or Latin.

He headed next to the military academy at Sandhurst to learn the art and science of soldiering. It was the first time he enjoyed his education. Later in the army, when posted to Bangalore, he finally found the time to compensate for his literary deficit. He had his mother send him volumes of Macaulay and Gibbon, which, along with *Bartlett's Familiar Quotations*, became his favorite guidebooks. His own writing style was, as he put it, "a combination of . . . the

staccato antitheses of the former and the rolling sentences and geni-
tival endings of the latter," to which "I stuck in a bit of my own from
time to time." The resulting composite resembled that of Dr. Johnson
in its "solemn facetiousness," as Isaiah Berlin has described it. Churchill probably would not have used a term like that.

In 1909 young Bertie followed his brother to the Royal Naval College
at Osborne. The school's motto, associated with Admiral Nelson,
was "There Is Nothing the Navy Cannot Do." His experience there
was as rough as one might imagine for a shy, awkward, and relatively
ignorant boy who had never been part of a society of his peers, let
alone a military one. His nicknames were Sardine, on account of his
size, and Bat Lugs, on account of his ears. There was also his stammer. He finished at the bottom of his class.

Bertie did not give up. He would, eventually, be recognized for
his "grit and 'never say I'm beaten' spirit." But he was no student.
During this time, his grandfather died. Now his father was the king.

In 1911 he entered another naval college, at Dartmouth. His
experience there would be happier. Particular highlights were the
chance to meet Churchill, then First Lord of the Admiralty, and
even to socialize with Mrs. Churchill. Others were his first ven-
tures at sea, including a memorable trip to the Caribbean and Canada in 1913. Bertie's shyness and stammer seemed to evaporate on
this journey. He received his appointment as a midshipman that
September, and followed his father into the navy.

Whereas much of the script of Bertie's life had been written for him
already, Winston's path had to be written largely by himself. For
while the life of the former was about to be challenged at home and

abroad in ways that nobody foresaw, the life of the latter—a life of constant, self-willed adventure—would not succeed by blending and flouting prescribed roles so easily. Events would alter the plan and pattern, such as they were. But they, too, needed a script.

Although born nearly a generation apart and of very different parentage, Winston and Bertie held some important things in common. Both were the sons of illustrious yet mixed families. Both from their earliest years failed to live up to certain expectations and were placed under great social and family pressure. Both suffered from indifferent, at some level at least, parents. Both had difficult fathers whom they nonetheless admired and in Winston's case worshipped. Both of their mothers were elegant but remote, and both were reared mainly by governesses. Both had physical limitations and were often ill and sought ways to compensate, either by persistent adaptation or by sheer bravery. Both had awkward associations with other boys and very few friends. Both were more or less young loners and lived to some degree in fantasy worlds of their own making. Both found difficulty in learning and in speaking. Both found some solace in an early military education, and later found relief, even exhilaration, in military combat. And while both differed in the degree to which they as young men sought glory and power in a public career, both had been born and reared during the height of the British Empire, when it was expected that anyone of their rank would do his duty to his country, no matter what.

CHAPTER THREE
Ordeals of Youth

The next half decade of Churchill's life after Sandhurst was, with the possible exception of the Second World War, the most satisfying. The reason was that he was always active, even hyperactive, and seemed to be going in a forward direction, despite many twists and turns. "Twenty to twenty-five! These are the years!" he later put it. As it happened, they coincided with Britain's imperial apogee. "It's a pushing age," he told his mother, "and we must shove with the best."

The complement of youthful feistiness is indelicacy. Churchill possessed both. There was the instance as a young second lieutenant when he turned up late to a royal dinner party. The entire party awaited his arrival in silence. It may have set a precedent. Edward VII had been close to Churchill's mother and had followed his career, especially his writing, with some appreciation, but there were other moments when Churchill seemed well out of favor. In the spring of 1906, King Edward wrote to his son: "As for Mr. Churchill he is *almost more* of [a] cad in office than he was in opposition," a verdict with which the prince, later George V, concurred.

Undaunted, Churchill drew a particular lesson from such events: standing out was a prerequisite to notoriety. Making this work on the battlefield took some effort. His first moments of combat were in Cuba, where he had volunteered as a war correspondent. There, he said, the main thing he learned was how best to duck fire.

These qualities—the thirst for glory and the desire to live to the fullest—have often been depicted as a form of warmongering. It was more complex than this. It was true that Churchill had a romantic attachment to combat, but it was a means to an end, which was the fulfillment of his chosen destiny. He was not bloodthirsty and did not seek war for its own sake. War was just another form of grand competition, albeit a rather dire and costly one. So, too, was politics.

Life for him in the army was not perfect. His fellow soldiers did not always appreciate him. According to contemporaries, he was a "Medal-hunter," a "Self-advertiser," and a "poisonous young man." All were partly true. War had won Churchill literary fame. His series of military adventures and mishaps—including a dramatic capture and escape during the Boer War—began the legend.

> You've heard of Winston Churchill;
> This is all I need to say—
> He's the latest and the greatest
> Correspondent of the day.

So began his long literary career as a raconteur and historian. About this and earlier adventures in Cuba, India, and Africa, he wrote brilliantly. His books and articles sold very well. He profited from speaking tours, especially in the United States, where he was once introduced as his country's future prime minister.

Life for Bertie in the navy was rather different from Winston's in the army. He was a good but not an enthusiastic sailor, having great affection for the navy but not for the sea. Sailing made him ill. His service was interrupted frequently by leaves on account of his poor health, including ulcers and other illnesses: appendicitis and dyspepsia. He was nervous at first but soon got along with his fellow midshipmen. He was with them, on board HMS *Collingwood*, when Archduke Franz Ferdinand was assassinated in 1914. They did not make much of the event; more noteworthy, according to Bertie's diary, was the visit of several girls from a nearby school. He probably never imagined the assassination would result in war. But his father worried. To his son, he wrote: "It has all come so suddenly. . . . Always do your duty. May God bless & protect you my dear boy is the earnest prayer of your very devoted Papa. . . . You can be sure that you are constantly in my thoughts."

Bertie's illnesses kept him away from much wartime action, a relief to his family but a cause of great frustration to him. He was eventually allowed back in time for the Battle of Jutland. His elder brother, the Prince of Wales, on the other hand, never saw action during the war, being assigned to the western front but kept far from the front lines. Not so Bertie. His ship was the first to open fire in the battle. He manned one of its five turrets.

"What the hell are you doing out there?" an officer demanded, having seen him climb onto the roof of the gun turret. "Come down before you get your head blown off." Inside, the air "was poisonous with the fumes of burnt cordite and of hot oil, and the smell of paint blistering on overheated guns." The "shells shrieked by. . . ."

"Whew, that was a near thing . . . ," Bertie said to his shipmate, "[t]he blighters have straddled us."

He was "distinctly startled and jumped down the hole in the top of the turret like a shot rabbit!!"

He survived, and was glad he had not felt more fear and that he had not made any big mistake. Just as well, his father was pleased. Young Bertie had quickly become, according to one of his shipmates, a hardened man.

Had he been of better health, and had he had a different elder brother or a different father, he might have made a good career as a naval officer. He would not have enjoyed it nearly as much as others, namely his father, might have, but it probably would have been a success. Had Winston been of a different disposition, and had he had superiors who were less hostile to him, he might have made a worthy career in the army. He, too, would have enjoyed it, most likely.

Neither was to be.

That the dramatic events of these years nonetheless toughened each man there can be little doubt. There was more: molding, shaping, and polishing. This happened as much by experience as by example: Bertie of his father, mainly, and of his navy commanders and comrades; and Churchill, once he entered politics, of his party and its leaders. Each man learned as much what to do as what not to do. They, especially Churchill, made mistakes, but it was the proximity to those of others in wartime that probably influenced them the most. They had earned their war medals, their spurs. They had seen so many of their best contemporaries disappear, so "many a pearl . . . which will never now be roped." They could face another war, knowing that they had done all their positions allowed them to do during the previous war and that they had not shirked their duty. They learned how and how not to relate to generals and admirals. They learned the necessity, and the limits, of bravery. Ultimately war was fatal to neither man, and for each it became an education. It probably made them stronger. It certainly made them smarter, and maybe wiser.

Churchill had entered Parliament in 1900 on the coattails of his war reporting. His marriage to Clementine Hozier seven years later was a success, the point at which, in the final words of his memoir of early life, he "married and lived happily ever afterwards." Their parents had been unfaithful, but they, so far as we know, never were. They had four children, the precise number to have, as Churchill later advised, "one to reproduce your wife, one to reproduce yourself, one for the increase in population, and one in case of accident." There would have been five had one daughter, Marigold, not died in infancy.

Political success bred more success at first: Churchill's tenure in Parliament began loudly as he established himself there as a vocal and pugnacious member, especially on military subjects. By his thirties he had replaced his father as the Churchill whose name most people knew.

However, his relations with his fellow Conservatives had soured to so great an extent, and his views had diverged so much with theirs, that he decided to switch parties, a rare thing to do for an ambitious novice politician. His timing turned out to be good—the Liberals carried the election of 1906. Try as he might, though, a liberal he was not. His instincts included a democratic strain, but not the "reluctance which inhibits Liberals from invoking force to solve a problem." He was really an old-fashioned conservative, as time would tell. He not only revered tradition but also viewed skeptically the idea of progress, at least in human nature. English conservatism better suited his disposition, perhaps, but not his political temperament, and just as before, he would find himself outside the mainstream of his own party and mistrusted by its principal brokers. When he switched parties again in 1924, some remembered calling him the "Blenheim rat." Well, "you could rat but you couldn't re-rat." It took a rare politician, Churchill later said, to get away with it. As both he and Bertie would learn, a man can still exert tremendous influence from the margins. Whether it could be converted into a central position was another question, one that would be answered as much by the course of events as by his inherent character and drive. For all that Churchill was regarded as an irrepressible opportunist, he was more like the future king in his capacity to fulfill a certain expectation, to do what was expected of him (and in Churchill's case, what was expected was not always favorable), once circumstances placed him in a particular position. His childhood and young adulthood allowed him to hone a talent for responding to challenges more than for seizing opportunities, per se. The same may have been true, though to a very different extent and in very different circumstances, of the future king, who did not appear to make many choices of his own. "Rising to the challenge" is a convenient cliché. In these two cases, it may be taken literally. So, too, is "two steps forward, one step back," although in Churchill's case the Snakes and Ladders metaphor in time became more apt.

In 1910, Churchill received his first cabinet department, the Home Office, becoming its youngest secretary in nearly a century. It was one of many government positions he would hold during the coming years. It brought the ambitious, hyperactive young politician into even closer contact with the monarch, now George V. He had effectively, though recklessly in the view of some critics, led the effort to defeat a libel against the king for an alleged secret marriage. He also acquired the duty of reporting regularly to the king the proceedings of the cabinet, a job generally done by the prime minister. "Churchill . . . approached the task with gusto," Roy Jenkins has written. "The whole exercise encapsulated his attitude to the monarchy: a great respect . . . combined with a total confidence and freedom in the expression of his own views on a basis of Whiggish equality." This may have been overstating the case. Was it really one of equality or an equitable division of labor? Churchill the Whig, if he could be called one, ascribed more value to the status of monarchy than to the substance; that is, the monarch must reign but not rule.

Churchill's opinion of the aristocracy, by contrast, was more forthright. He welcomed its eclipse and warned that throwing it a lifeline would lead to a dangerous national sclerosis. This was most likely not the result of self-hatred or clear-cut class bias. His disdain for his fellow members of the aristocracy could be said to match his regard for the middle, particularly the lower-middle, class, but Churchill had little patience for class warriors from among the so-called lower orders. They were not spared the show of his antagonism. There was the Sidney Street incident, in which he, as Home Secretary, personally intervened in an attack upon a group of anarchists and annoyed colleagues by having his photograph from the scene appear in the newspaper. Churchill achieved several things as Home Secretary—notably prison reform—but it was the exhibitionism that most people remembered. Sidney Street and the Welsh Tonypandy riots in late 1910, when troops threatened to put down a miners' strike, stuck in the mind.

Being offered a proper military department the following year must have come as a relief. Now thirty-seven, he relished the job of First Lord of the Admiralty. British naval power, he later wrote, was the center of British existence, not merely a source for expansion, as it was for Germany. The Admiralty may have been the most important government department during what many people presumed at the time would be a short, intense war, fought largely between gunships where the British with their new dreadnoughts were sure to prove victorious. But a quick victory was not to be. The First World War would bring more death and suffering than the British people had ever expected. Churchill ended it with the title of chancellor of the Duchy of Lancaster, which David Lloyd George had said was "reserved either for beginners in the Cabinet or for distinguished politicians who had reached the first stages of unmistakable decrepitude." Churchill managed to achieve both in record time.

The reason was the terrible Dardanelles campaign in 1915. Scores of men were lost in a doomed attempt to expel the Turks from the Dardanelles as the prelude to seizing Constantinople. He had been a passionate advocate of the campaign and helped to prevail against others who were less enthusiastic. Its failure was not entirely Churchill's fault, and much of the responsibility fell on the army, but Churchill was the man most identified with it. His idea had been that this action against Germany's Turkish ally could succeed. It was unlikely. But it made great sense to him at the time. Churchill blamed the military commanders, and not for the first time, for faulty execution of an otherwise sound, albeit ambitious, plan.

Now, as Roy Jenkins has written, the "littorals were covered with the bones of those who had fallen in 1915, and also with the skeleton of his early and considerable reputation." Churchill was pilloried. About the only person to express sympathy was his old army adversary Lord Kitchener, even though he probably bore as much blame for the Dardanelles disaster as Churchill did. "There is one thing at least they can never take from you," he told him. "When the War began you had the Fleet ready." Yes, at least one historian has asked, "[b]ut what precisely was it ready *for*?"

The recovery of Churchill's reputation, for one. It would take time. The failure fueled the perception of a reckless and dangerous mountebank. Sidney Street and Tonypandy had been unfortunate excesses of exuberance; the Dardanelles action was a tragic disaster. As before, he turned to the inner resource of self-assurance, some would say egocentricity, which saw him through such crises, yet had the tendency to bring them on in the first place. He admitted, in other words, the fact but not the necessity of failure. Sharing a Turkish bath with his friend Duff Cooper, Churchill insisted that he would be vindicated by the commission of enquiry and would have a new job in due course. "He is a strange creature," Cooper concluded.

Churchill presently went to the western front to command an infantry battalion. He saw some combat but otherwise succeeded in raising morale by delousing his troops and by instituting the practice of singing on the march. He showed his usual bravery but was also reckless: "For God's sake keep still, sir!" "Put out that bloody light." These were typical cries heard from the trenches while Churchill was there. He was known for ordering nighttime artillery attacks, for example, which had the effect of angering not only the enemy but his own troops as well. But he emerged unscathed. The same could not be said of his career. Although he returned to government in 1917 as minister of munitions, gaining valuable knowledge of the latest advances in weaponry, followed by service as secretary of state for war, for air, and, finally, for the colonies, he lost his seat in 1922, joining the Communist candidate in his Durham constituency at the bottom of the list. Kept out of much of the campaign by an operation, he contributed the memorable line "In the twinkling of an eye, I found myself without an office, without a seat, without a Party and without an appendix."

Another organ has been mentioned less kindly: he was simply "a floating kidney in the body politic," drawn in two directions by his dual nature as conservative adventurer, being "both cautious and wild by turns." He tried to turn his mind away from current politics and instead to writing, including an excellent history of the war. Churchill may have been a likable outcast to some, but there was no doubting his condition. He was in the wilderness.

Bertie had had a rather different war. On his twenty-first birthday, the king made him a Knight of the Garter, a distinct honor and, apparently, a vote of confidence in his son. He would return to the navy after his convalescence, seeing more action—including a U-boat attack that brought him face to face with human death—until his health again forced him out. He would spend the rest of the war in England, apart from a quick visit to France soon before the end while seconded to the new Royal Air Force. He received flying lessons and, eventually, certification.

He went on to perform the duties of a young prince and continued to learn from his father. The period gave him useful practice, particularly in visiting hospitals, soon to become a royal staple. News of it reached as far as the United States, where Franklin Roosevelt later told the story of George V noticing "a huge tattoo" on top of an injured man's chest. The king

> asked what it was, to which the man had said: "It is Your Majesty, sir." The King made him open his shirt and the man showed him not only himself, but on the top of his back, Queen Mary, and on each arm the Prince of Wales and Princess Mary. The King congratulated him on his patriotism, to which the man replied: "That isn't all, sir; whenever I sits down I sits on Kaiser Bill and von Hindenburg"!

In June 1920 the king named his son the Duke of York, which had been his own former title, and set for him an expanding program of royal duties. Bertie also developed a few special interests, notably in factories, so that his brothers called him "the Foreman." He probably did not mind; to him this was more than royal busywork. Then, in 1923, he scored an even greater success with his marriage to Elizabeth Bowes-Lyon. It nearly did not happen but did thanks to a friend, J. C. C. Davidson, who girded him with the will to propose, which he had thought he could not do. She accepted on the third attempt. The two had laid eyes on each other at a tea given at Spencer House, owned by Churchill's cousin. It was their second meeting but their first as young adults. She had been hesitant during the courtship, and there had been another suitor, whom it was said Queen Mary had helped to remove from the competition. The two developed their own affectionate language, known as the "mutual telegram" in the shape of a smile, and began a most successful marriage.

Once again his father was gratified. "By your quiet useful work you have endeared yrself to the people," he wrote to him. "I am quite certain that Elizabeth will be a splendid partner." This was an understatement. The duke's marriage, wrote his official biographer, was nothing less than the "first great climacteric of his life . . . it brought him much for which he had long craved in deprivation— love, understanding, sympathy, support . . . and his whole conspectus of life changed accordingly." She was the primary source of his strength from then on, according to most accounts, and also helped to ease relations with his larger family by becoming a favored confidante of his brothers. All this greatly pleased the king, who reaffirmed Bertie's position as favorite son.

They took up residence in the small White Lodge in Richmond Park. Daughter Elizabeth was born in 1926 and Margaret Rose in 1930. It was the duke's private happiness with his own immediate family that girded him in public. He was much aided by his wife, who also supervised his parenting, for example, when instructing him never to shout at his daughters as his own father had done with him, thereby "making you feel uncomfortable [and losing] all your real affection."

He did not need to be loved by millions of subjects; he now had all the love he appeared to want from his own tiny circle. The confidence that this particular source of security granted made it possible, and even probable, that the two would combine in strength, allowing Bertie to further the familial role that his father and great-grandmother had promoted so assiduously. This was doing as well as being. He said upon his return from Australia and New Zealand in July 1927:

> I return a thorough optimist. When one has travelled over the vast extent of the Empire; when one has witnessed what our fathers have accomplished; when one has seen how the grit and creative purpose of our kinsmen have triumphed over the most tremendous difficulties, it is impossible to despair of the future of the British race. The same qualities which carried us successfully through the war will, I am convinced, so long as we remain united as members of one family, enable us to surmount all difficulties that may beset us, however formidable or however perplexing.

In November 1928, King George V became ill and began a prolonged decline lasting another seven years, so long, in fact, that when the end finally came at the beginning of 1936, Bertie was caught by surprise: "What's all this about the King not being well?" The duke and his elder brother, the Prince of Wales, returned to Buckingham Palace, though the latter, who had been visiting Africa, took longer to get there. "I am going to bag the Throne in your absence!!!!" the duke joked. The king died on January 20. The prince broke down in his mother's arms, screaming and crying. She responded by kissing his hand the moment her husband was gone. Thus began the most difficult period in Bertie's life.

CHAPTER FOUR

Abdication

The interwar years—Churchill called a portion of them "the Loaded Pause"—were fateful for both men. Bertie would marry, have children, and endure the worst crisis to befall the British monarchy in recent memory. By the end of 1936 he would be king. Churchill, having found himself again on the margins, again recovered. He would reenter government, once more as a Conservative, having earlier concluded that "Liberalism was a state of mind rather than a growing political force," only to be sidelined by the prime minister, Stanley Baldwin. Again, he would see his career and reputation founder.

One reason this time around was his loyalty to King Edward VIII. Churchill was the most prominent, perhaps the only, Tory to do so well after it was politic or useful. The unhappy royal may have known better: "I want no more of this Princing!" he was overheard to say before his coronation, adding, "I want to be an ordinary person" and "I suppose the fact of the matter is that I'm quite the wrong sort of person to be Prince of Wales." To his brother Bertie he later said something similar: "It was never in my scheme of things to be King of England."

Or he may have prepared for it and may well have intended to keep it. A monarch with a loose reputation was nothing new. Edward was said to take after his free-spirited grandfather, who followed in the wake of so many decades of the reign of the staid Queen Victoria, so much so that the term "Victorian" will forever carry the association of dark rooms, tight collars and corsets, and large, virtuous families. Stern, strict, and dutiful George V, who followed Edward VII, brought about a kind of restoration, and his son, too, may have been expected to perpetuate the cycle.

The twentieth century has been described with good reason as the age of extremes. The new king declared that his bachelor days were over and that he was now determined to marry an American, Wallis Simpson, "a nice, quiet, well-bred mouse of a woman with large startled eyes and a huge mole." The problem was that she was a divorcée who was still married to her second husband when this latest association began. Edward could not remain on the throne if he were married to such a person. There could be no doubt of that. His determination to impose his beloved Wallis upon the British people and to demand her acceptance took things too far. He was her "absolute slave," and was unmovable. He even began to speak with a slight American accent. He cared little for the concerns of those around him and even less for the popular press. Both were errors. "The Battle for the Throne," meanwhile, "had begun." Its partisans were not only journalists but also figures like Sibyl Colefax, the *salonnière* hostess whose circle, it was said, was "a party of lunatics presided over by an efficient, trained hospital nurse," and her chief rival, Emerald Cunard, whose circle was "a party of lunatics presided over by a lunatic." So formidable was the mobilization of gossip by these people that they and others like them were seen to be the arbiters of a royal split. The king's loyal but dwindling camp began to wonder how much longer the ordeal could drag out. The Canadian press tycoon Lord Beaverbrook foretold the end to the Anglo-American social adventurer Chips Channon:

"Our cock would be all right if only he would fight, but at the moment he will not even crow."

"Cocks crow better in the morning."

"Not this one."

Churchill, however, stood by Edward. "What crime . . . had the King committed?" he asked. "Had we not sworn allegiance to him? Were we not bound to that oath? Was he to be condemned unheard? Was he seeking to do anything that was not permitted to the meanest of his subjects?"

Why did Churchill do it? At that time, he was a man of known qualities, but he was also tenaciously, even permanently, unpredictable. There was no record of hostility, true enough, and Churchill was a loyal monarchist. He and his father had not always seen eye to eye with their respective sovereigns and, in the latter's case, had even reached the point of a public breach. Yet Churchill was said to like this king, a "chatty, handy type of monarch," and had been close to him socially. Churchill was consistent about many things, and inconsistent about others, but the one value from which he never wavered was his reverence for the institution of the monarchy, and this now included defending the flawed man on the throne. Churchill's real feelings were probably mixed, as suggested by his later confession to Beaverbrook: "Perhaps we were both wrong that time." He may well have placed Edward in a different category. Or this may be reading too much between the lines. Once, during a game of bridge, "Winston, having led up to and sacrificed his king, declared: 'Nothing is here for tears. The king cannot fall unworthily if he falls to the sword of the ace.'"

A less charitable view of the crisis has held that this had nothing, or at least very little, to do with whom the king married or bedded and everything to do with Churchill's own political ambitions and corresponding strategies. By 1930, if not earlier, Churchill had cast his lot decidedly against Baldwin, "the cabin-boy made captain," who became determined to see abdication through as rapidly as possible after a difficult delay. There was no love lost between them. Churchill considered Baldwin, along with Joseph Chamberlain, father of Neville, to have had the most devastating effect on the country of any two politicians. It is probably impossible to disentangle Churchill's motives, although given the result—it would coincide with his longest period in the wilderness, lasting over a decade—it was more likely that he wished the king to survive more than he wished Baldwin to fall. In any case, "to bugger Baldwin," as Beaverbrook (who genuinely did seek Baldwin's defeat) put it, was not entirely consistent with Churchill's nature. Baldwin, "half Machiavelli, half Milton," had brought some of this on himself, pretending for too long that the crisis was not really happening, then wishing it away at the final moment by taking an absolute position in favor of abdication, more or less concurrent with the king's own ultimatum over his decision regarding Mrs. Simpson. "Let this thing be settled between you and me alone," the king was supposed to have said to him. "I don't want outside interference." By then this was out of the question. Churchill was not the only one who "had put himself in a false position." Baldwin "flung up his hand. 'We are all in false positions!' " The final position was, Wallis or the throne. That is certainly not the way Churchill would have preferred it, for while his loyalty to the king was clear, he never took seriously the possibility of Wallis becoming queen. He dismissed whatever power she had, which was considerable. Nor had Bertie publicly admitted the possibility that his brother would not become and remain king. At the very least, he never expected it to happen so soon.

Bertie endured the entire episode with "unrelieved gloom." His brother had barely spoken to him, or confided in him, and rarely sought his opinion. This was probably for the best, since Bertie would have had to support his brother even more aggressively than he had done. Nonetheless, he, as well as Elizabeth, especially, had deplored the prospect of the "shop-soiled American, with two living husbands and a voice like a rusty saw" being anywhere near their family, let alone a member of it.

His brother's neglect must have been agonizing. Despite their differences, the two had been close their entire lives. How often he must have thought, as his wife once said to an acquaintance, "You are a lucky man to be able to do what you like." But she stiffened the spine, as she so often did: "I have great faith in Bertie," she wrote to Queen Mary. "He sees very straight, & if this terrible responsibility comes to him he will face it bravely." For now he did, even while being ignored. He and Wallis were the two most strident, unwavering opponents of abdication. Then at last, on December 7, he heard from the king.

"Come & see me after dinner."

"No, I will come & see you at once." The awful & ghastly suspense of waiting was over. I found him pacing up & down the room, & he told me his decision that he would go. I went back to the Royal Lodge for dinner & returned to the Fort [Belvedere] later. I felt having once got there I was not going to leave. As he is my eldest brother I had to be there to try & help him in his hour of need.

When recounting this to his mother, he "sobbed like a child." The short signing ceremony took place on the tenth. "Perfectly calm D signed 5 or 6 copies of the instrument & then 5 copies of his message to Parliament, one for each Dominion Parliament. It was a dreadful moment & one never to be forgotten by those present."

The family gathered for dinner the following day. "When D & I said good-bye we kissed, parted as freemasons & he bowed to me as his King." The performance was as unfamiliar as it was uncomfortable. "All my ancestors succeeded to the throne after their predecessors had died. Mine is not only alive, but very much so."

Edward had abdicated and a new King George—the Sixth—took his place. To his brother's onetime partisan, he wrote:

My dear Mr. Churchill,

I am writing to thank you for your very nice letter to me. I know how devoted you have been, and still are, to my dear brother, and I feel touched beyond words by your sympathy and understanding in the very difficult problems that have arisen since he left us in December. I fully realise the great responsibilities and cares that I have taken on as King, and I feel most encouraged to receive your good wishes, as one of our great statesmen, and from one who has served his country so faithfully. I can only hope and trust that the good feeling and hope that exists in the Country and Empire now will prove a good example to other Nations in the world.

"This gesture of magnanimity," Churchill later recalled, "towards one whose influence at that time had fallen to zero will ever be a cherished experience in my life."

The king had a difficult time of it at first. "Dickie," he said to his cousin, "this is absolutely terrible. I never wanted this to happen; I'm quite unprepared for it." Mountbatten tried to reassure him by quoting something his own father had said to Bertie's: "George, you're wrong. There is no more fitting preparation for a King than to have been trained in the Navy." Baldwin also assured him that he had the country's full support.

The coronation took place on May 12, 1937. "I could eat no breakfast, and had a sinking feeling inside," Bertie wrote. He later told someone "that for long periods . . . he was unaware of what was happening." Yet, as Channon has described,

[t]he panorama was splendid, and we felt we were sitting in a frame, for the built-up stands suggested Ascot, or perhaps— more romantically—the tournaments of mediaeval days; the chairs were covered with blue velvet . . . on all sides were MPs I knew and their be-plumed, be-veiled, be-jewelled wives. . . .

The North Transept was a vitrine of bosoms and jewels and bobbing tiaras. . . . There was an excited pause, then a hush as the regalia was carried in and then out again. . . . And I looked about again, dazzled by the red, the gilt, the gold, the grandeur. After a little the real Royalties arrived, the Princess Royal looking cross, the tiny Princesses excited by their coronets and trains, and the two Royal Duchesses looking staggering. . . . Another pause, till the gaunt Queen of Norway appeared, followed by Queen Mary, ablaze, regal and over-powering. Then the Queen's procession, and she appeared, dignified but smiling and much more bosomy. Then, so surrounded by dignitaries carrying wands, sceptres, orbs and staffs, as to be overshadowed, George VI himself. He carried himself well.

Churchill came out of the abdication less well. Having broken with his fellow Conservatives, especially Baldwin, a half decade before, he found himself at the nadir of his party, and with no cabinet role.

Out of Office! And what a variety of Office he had seen. The crowded career is too familiar to need rehearsal in any detail. . . . Under-Secretary of State for the Colonies, President of the Board of Trade, Home Secretary, First Lord of the Admiralty, Chancellor of the Duchy of Lancaster, Minister of Munitions, Secretary of State for War, Secretary of State for Air, Secretary of State for the Colonies, Chancellor of the Exchequer—all these lay behind him by 1930, interspersed and accompanied, outside the field of politics, by one or two Lord Rectorships, active service and prolific authorship.

Again, the pliable Churchill recovered. His position vis-à-vis the reconstituted royals would improve when he stood by the new king in the decision to deny a royal title to Mrs. Simpson. It probably did not dispel the Baldwin-related suspicions—which Baldwin himself may have fueled when he met secretly with Bertie on the eve of the abdication. This also is unknowable. What is known is that a much different man now wore the crown. Buckingham Palace was occupied by a charming and attractive young family. The wholesome Georgian monarchy was restored. The country could relax. The people could feel confident and hopeful.

There was still the matter of the king himself: he had not sought this enormous new job, however much the prospect of having it may have sat in the back of his mind. He must have been frightened, yet part of him seemed well armored. As was now his custom, he began to swim harder and faster once he survived the initial shock of being thrown into deep water. He would not be a figurehead. Yet he was not, at least not then, at all temperamentally suited to rule.

How far they had come in a mere two decades. Churchill lurked in the political wilderness, not entirely in disgrace but close to it, "an Ishmael in public life." The king—who was not yet king and had few premonitions of becoming one—was a shy young man who dreaded speaking in public and found the first few episodes when forced to do so to be excruciating. Having become king, he was said to have "discovered that he was for the first time in his life able to make up his own mind." By 1940 the two would lead the nation together in war.

If their upbringing and youth had set the foundation for the men they would become, the interwar years thrust them together in a way that would allow each one to master the forward elements of his character. For Churchill these were his tenacity and his power of rejuvenation; for the king it was his decency, integrity, and duty. In time some elements of each merged with those of the other. Whereas these qualities in both men were praiseworthy but perhaps ill suited to the 1920s, by the mid-1930s events and circumstances would create an entirely different need for them.

The interwar crises had a silver lining. That is to say, neither man emerged unscathed or undamaged from setbacks, but both acted to master them. Some part of their character drove them on, even against, particularly in the king's case, his evident desires. He was not ambitious, at least not in public. At first he would be a reluctant monarch. He was the good, loyal second son, pleased with his place in the immediate background. And why should he not have been?

Churchill, on the other hand, could not have been happy with subordination. He meant to be the leading man or no man. He was no mere careerist; the role he sought was historic; it was meant to transcend, to last well beyond, his professional career. And so his tactical pursuits went, at least in these years, somewhat against the grain of the man on the make and would seem, on first examination, to be rather self-destructive. Whereas the soon-to-be king would spend the remainder of the decade gaining further in confidence, Churchill would spend it tempering his ambition with what he may have considered to be self-willed judiciousness, or as near to that as he could come.

CHAPTER FIVE

Appeasement

The 1930s "was the Devil's decade. It came in like a ravening wolf, and went out like a roaring lion. It began with a world in economic chaos, and ended with the world at war." Like Churchill's description of the German drive to rearm, it was "invested with a ruthless, lurid tinge. It glittered and it glared."

Churchill was at one of the lowest points in his public career. He became entangled on the wrong side of the abdication question. He would be on the right side of "appeasement," though here he went against the popular grain. He remained a member of Parliament but had not held cabinet office since 1929; the leaders of his party, including both prime ministers, Baldwin and Chamberlain, held him in contempt. His close supporters in the high reaches of his party, it was said, could fit into a small smoking room. The remainder of the Conservatives, by contrast, were, as the saying went, merely Tories who were ashamed of themselves. According to many of them, Churchill had been a brilliant comet whose trajectory had long since fallen below the horizon. He resumed painting and writing; he brooded; he simmered. But "like the chamomile, the more he is trodden on, the more he flourishes." Only just not yet. For now the savior of British honor and strength was the prime minister, Neville Chamberlain.

During his years in the wilderness, Churchill wrote his four-volume biography of Marlborough and studied his ancestor's military imagination. He must have thought many times what it would take to lead a similar Grand Alliance. He also worried about the need arising for it. Churchill was the only man, according to his doomed friend from the Foreign Office, Ralph Wigram, who "has always, always understood." Wigram was the informant who "clung to [him] like a drowning man to a spar" and who provided the secret intelligence showing the extent of German rearmament and plans, right up to his premature and mysterious death—some said from illness, others suicide—in December 1936.

Churchill had been right about Germany. He was right about the weakness of his country's armed forces, right about Hitler, right about Chamberlain and appeasement, and right about the stakes for Britain and her empire. No other major political figure detected the immediate future so clearly, or appeared to have so accurate a perception of the mood and capacities of his country, save Hitler himself, probably because the Führer spent so much time reading foreign newspapers and ignoring much of the expert advice that was offered to him. Churchill knew well, as the diplomatic diarist Harold Nicolson put it, that the "British people, in fact, have for years been the victims of too little information and too many phrases. . . . They crooned themselves to sleep with the lullaby of 'collective security.' . . . How sane; how sensible; how sinuous; how sound!" The challenge was to avoid being dubbed a Cassandra and to find some way to do something about it.

If the king were thrust into performing a role he said he had never wanted, Churchill thrust himself into the part he had always aimed to play. The king was bound by duty and the desperation of his family, the country, and the institution during a crisis that never should have happened but was predictable and predicted, most of all by Churchill. Although neither man would have been fully aware of it, both, again, found themselves in the right places at the right moment. Imagine if Edward had remained on the throne, even without a Queen Wallis, with appeasement in the air and his integrity thrown into question. The charge against him (and even more so, against her) of Nazi sympathy was exaggerated and probably unfounded, but it was there nonetheless. It did not apply to his younger brother, who, by contrast, had served under fire in the last war and was married to a woman who lost a brother in it. German heritage notwithstanding, there was no love lost for Nazis anywhere in George VI's household. The public knew this as well as they knew Churchill's own sympathies.

The story actually was not so simple. In the end, according to Nicolson, it had been Halifax more than anyone else who, as foreign secretary, swayed this king from his loyalty to Chamberlain, under whom Halifax served, and to the "dual policy of resistance and conciliation" that they had designed. It is not easy to disaggregate the prime minister's character and intentions, and he was not the only guilty party. Chamberlain, in fact, was a more complicated figure whose reputed malevolence, weakness, or incompetence lies in the eye of the beholder. "Do not mind overmuch the attribution of false motive," Baldwin liked to say. But Chamberlain has yet to overcome the verdict of posterity: that he really was the wrong man in the wrong place at the wrong time.

In early 1939 in London, Halifax unveiled a large map of Europe and said, "What a bloody place it is." The scars there had only just begun to heal—and to heal badly, in that the scar tissue was a thin one of idealism, escapism, even hedonism, followed by cynicism. Cynicism makes a poor alloy. It divides and it dilutes. An "avenging march of the mediocrities" was under way. How easy, then, is it to dismiss or otherwise to succumb to an ahistorical depiction of the policy of appeasement?

The term "appeasement" reveals its linguistic root: peace. Nearly everyone was desperate to preserve it. George V had forewarned, "I am an old man. I have been through one world war. How can I go through another?" He repeated: "I will not have another war. *I will not.*" Chamberlain had perhaps erred in his tactics, but his effort was not irrational and certainly not unpopular. Nicolson has reflected the mood upon Chamberlain's return from Berchtesgaden in September 1938:

> When he said these words, "as a last resort," he whipped off his pince-nez and looked up at the skylight with an expression of grim hope. . . . "It was," he said with a wry grin, "my first flight," and then he described the whole visit as "this adventure." He said that his conversation with Hitler had convinced him that the Führer was prepared, on behalf of the Sudeten Germans, "to risk world war." As he said these words a shudder of horror passed through the House of Commons. . . . He raised his face so that the light from the ceiling fell full upon it. All the lines of anxiety and weariness seemed suddenly to have been smoothed out; he appeared ten years younger and

triumphant. "Herr Hitler," he said, "has just agreed to post-pone his mobilisation for twenty-four hours and to meet me in conference with Signor Mussolini and Monsieur Daladier at Munich."

First, complete silence. Then an eruption of joy. Nicolson remembered it as "one of the most dramatic moments" he had "ever witnessed."

For most of his career in politics, Chamberlain did not conform to the umbrella-wielding caricature. He was rather a tough and sometimes principled politician who drove a hard bargain. People who met him noted his strong arms and gaze. The British Empire he led was still seen as powerful and permanent. When he touted the small piece of paper that brought "peace in our time," he most probably meant it. Yet he had never experienced the kinds of adversity known to either Churchill or the king. Whether this made him more naïve is not possible to know, but it may have made him less courageous and thoughtful. He had high powers of concentration but also a myopic quality when exercising them. "Injudicious they may have been, ignorant never." This was both an asset and a liability. "Indeed," Donald Cameron Watt has diagnosed, "that was precisely the trouble. So much of Chamberlain's thinking, so much of his analysis, was conditional, tentative, contingent. He doubted; but he was never certain. He distrusted; but he did not totally disbelieve." He was—in other both positive and negative terms—a small-minded person who excelled in a place like Birmingham in peacetime but was ill suited to lead the world's largest empire in war. The more out of depth he was, the more close-minded and stubborn he became.

For the moment, however, he inspired confidence. Channon, one of his biggest fans, was not alone: "Of course a way out will now be found. Neville by his imagination and practical good sense, has saved the world." Another Tory later commented, with reference to the security guarantee given to Poland, "You know, I am a trifle uneasy about this Polish agreement. It seems to me to imply a definite commitment on our part."

"I quite agree," replied his friend, "and we must thank heaven that we have Neville at the helm."

Others, not least the royal family, would agree. Chamberlain was in good standing with them. He slipped occasionally, as when the king was "royally displeased" by not having been warned of Anthony Eden's decision to resign in 1938 as foreign secretary over a disagreement on the timing of negotiations with Italy, one result being that the king became sympathetic toward Eden. That much was implied at least by Eden's memoirs. (This also was the only moment over which Churchill recalled losing sleep, including the entire period of the war.) Nevertheless, the king had cultivated so good a routine with his prime minister that the latter could regard himself as the royal couple's "Godfather." It is difficult to imagine a warm feeling between these two men and yet the king's letters to Chamberlain following his resignation seem heartfelt. He was sad to see him go. But we get ahead of the story.

The king could talk freely to Chamberlain, but the same was not true in reverse. It is also difficult to know the king's mind at this stage. Like many people, he probably did not know himself. "Everything is a maze," he had written back in September. The country seemed desperate to believe that Hitler could have his pound of flesh in the Sudetenland and be done. Perhaps the main cynic was

Hitler himself, who was said to believe that Britain was prepared to fight, just not anytime soon. Those who said otherwise, Churchill among them, were perceived to be a small, bellicose minority, also desperate to slay the guilty demons of the last war. Few wanted to hear what they had to say. This included both the king and the queen, and much of the royal family, who were about as pro-appeasement as one could be. Here, for example, is Queen Mary: "I am sure you feel as angry as I do at people croaking as they do at the P.M.'s action. . . . It is always so easy for people to criticise when they do not know the ins and outs of the question." And the king to the queen: "I wish [Chamberlain] could have got more out of him. . . . I don't much care for our new guarantees of the new Czechoslovakian frontier against unprovoked aggression. . . . What we want is a guarantee from Hitler that he won't walk into it in 3 or 4 months' time." Even so, the queen had written, "for even if nothing comes of it, [Chamberlain] will have made, in England's name, the beau geste for peace." She sent Halifax a copy of *Mein Kampf* and urged him to educate himself about Hitler—by skimming it. Many decades later, when asked if her views on Chamberlain had changed, she replied that they had not: "[W]hatever people say, [Munich] gave us that year . . . to rearm, and build a few aeroplanes."

Others no doubt saw matters differently. Churchill played the role of insurrectionist, warning "as familiar as the voice of a muezzin announcing the hour of prayer" about the peril his country faced from the Nazis. They posed much more than a political or military threat; the threat was a mortal one, to all civilization.

In the summer of 1938, Their Majesties traveled to France. They reviewed fifty thousand troops at Versailles and were impressed with the tanks, aircraft, and Moroccan cavalry they saw. As it happened, Churchill also spent a good part of the fateful year in France, including five weeks on the Riviera and again later in the year to coincide with the royal visit. For some time he had bemoaned the mood of his compatriots back home: "Chattering, busy, sporting, toiling, amused from day to day by headlines, and from night to night by cinemas, they can yet feel themselves slipping, sinking, rolling backward. . . . Stop it! Stop it!! Stop it now!! NOW is the appointed time." They persisted in pacifist delusion, promoting the "cause of disarmament" by "Mush, Slush and Gush." He called for more ships, more aircraft, more expenditure, more preparation.

His warnings were not well taken. He was accused of warmongering. Others greeted him with renewed taunts of "Mussolini!" recalling his earlier praise for Il Duce and his reluctance to condemn the attack on Abyssinia. Some may have wondered, in Channon's words, if "Winston, that fat, brilliant, unbalanced, illogical orator," was "more than just that. . . . Or is he perhaps right, banging his head against an uncomprehending country and unsympathetic government?"

On September 6, Chamberlain wrote to the king: "All the same I have a 'hunch,' as J. P. Morgan says, that we shall get through this time without the use of force." Only a week later he warned the king to "be prepared for the possibility of a sudden change for the worse."

The king in turn offered to send a peace feeler to Hitler, from "one ex-Serviceman to another." That idea was received skeptically by Halifax. Again, he suggested sending a peace feeler and was rebuffed, this time by Chamberlain. He offered to do this repeatedly not only with Hitler but also with others, like the Japanese. Each time, Chamberlain resisted.

Then, on September 16, Chamberlain went to the palace to brief the king on his latest talks with Hitler, ominously. He assured him that Hitler "was not bluffing" and that "only the intervention of his visit had held up the invasion of Czechoslovakia. He had won a breathing-space."

Finally, two weeks later—Munich. Chamberlain had received Hitler's assurance that there would be no war. The king greeted the returning Chamberlain eagerly, even happily. Chamberlain joined him and the queen on the balcony of Buckingham Palace and waved to the cheering crowds. Chamberlain's appearance on the balcony was a violation of protocol. But few people at the time seemed to care about that. Nor did they understand the consequences of what Chamberlain had done. "You might think that we had won a major victory instead of betraying a minor country," said a diplomat. "But I can bear anything as long as [Chamberlain] doesn't talk about peace with honour." Alas, he did, just a few minutes later.

In his October 2 broadcast, the king thanked the British people "for their calm resolve during these critical days, and for the readiness with which they responded to the different calls made upon them." Then he concluded, "After the magnificent efforts of the Prime Minister in the cause of peace, it is my fervent hope that a new era of friendship and prosperity may be dawning among the peoples of the world." He also proposed that Chamberlain give another broadcast calling for national service, presumably in preparation for war should all else fail. Chamberlain rejected it then, but he did it the following January.

What Churchill would have done in Chamberlain's stead is open to conjecture. The historian Gerhard Weinberg has claimed that back in June, Churchill "was privately telling the Prague government that if in office he would most likely follow the same policy." This neither was nor is the consensus view. In public now he spoke of "sustain[ing] a defeat without a war, the consequences of which will travel far with us along our road . . . the first sip, the first foretaste of a bitter cup which will be proffered to us year by year unless, by a supreme recovery of moral health and martial vigour, we arise again and take our stand for freedom as in the olden time."

Later, in a confrontation with U.S. ambassador Joseph P. Kennedy and the journalist Walter Lippmann, "waving his whisky-and-soda to mark his periods, stubbing his cigar with the other hand," Churchill underscored the point:

> It may be true, it may well be true, that this country will at the outset of this coming and to my mind almost inevitable war be exposed to dire peril and fierce ordeals. It may be true that steel and fire will rain down upon us day and night scattering death and destruction far and wide. It may be true that our sea-communications will be imperilled and our food-supplies placed in jeopardy. Yet these trials and disasters, I ask you to believe me Mr. Lippmann, will but serve to steel the resolution of the British people and to enhance our will for victory. . . . I for one would willingly lay down my life in combat, rather than, in fear of defeat, surrender to the menaces of these most sinister men. It will then be for you, for the Americans, to preserve and to maintain the great heritage of the English-speaking peoples. It will be for you to think imperially, which means to think always of something higher and more vast than one's national interests. Nor should I die happy

in the great struggle which I see before me, were I not convinced that if we in this dear dear island succumb to the ferocity and might of our enemies, over there in your distant and immune continent the torch of freedom will burn untarnished and (I trust and hope) undismayed.

He proved correct. Little less than a year later, Hitler invaded Poland and another war began. On the first of September the king resumed keeping a daily diary. On September 3 at 6:00 p.m., he delivered his war message by radio:

In this grave hour, perhaps the most fateful in our history, I send to every household of my peoples, both at home and overseas, this message, spoken with the same depth of feeling for each one of you as if I were able to cross your threshold and speak to you myself.

For the second time in the lives of most of us we are at war. Over and over again we have tried to find a peaceful way out of the differences between ourselves and those who are now our enemies. But it has been in vain. We have been forced into a conflict. For we are called, with our allies, to meet the challenge of a principle which, if it were to prevail, would be fatal to any civilised order in the world.

It is the principle which permits a State, in the selfish pursuit of power, to disregard its treaties and its solemn pledges; which sanctions the use of force, or threat of force, against the Sovereignty and independence of other States. Such a principle, stripped of all disguise, is surely the mere primitive doctrine that Might is Right. And if this principle were established throughout the world, the freedom of our own country and of the whole British Commonwealth of Nations would be in danger. But far more than this—the peoples of the world would be kept in the bondage of fear, and all hopes of settled peace and of the security of justice and liberty among nations would be ended.

This is the ultimate issue which confronts us. For the sake of all that we ourselves hold dear, and of the world's order and peace, it is unthinkable that we should refuse to meet the challenge.

It is to this high purpose that I now call my people at home and my peoples across the Seas, who will make our cause their own. I ask them to stand calm and firm and united in this time of trial. The task will be hard. There may be dark days ahead, and war can no longer be confined to the battlefield. But we can only do the right as we see the right, and reverently commit our cause to God. If one and all we keep resolutely faithful to it, ready for whatever service or sacrifice it may demand, then, with God's help, we shall prevail.

May He bless and keep us all.

In his diary he added, "Today we are at War again, & I am no longer a midshipman in the Royal Navy."

The calculated game of appeasement had ended. Now came the Phony War, the period of several months in which a state of war existed but without military engagement. It was not clear what the government's strategy was. Chamberlain described it as a wait-and-see policy of deterrence. "My own belief is that we shall win," he wrote to Franklin Roosevelt, "not by a complete and spectacular military victory, which is unlikely under modern conditions, but by convincing the Germans that they cannot win." Did this make sense? Someone in the Foreign Office put it this way:

An elderly gentleman with gout,
When asked what the war was about,
In a Written Reply,
Said, "My colleagues and I
Are doing our best to find out."

The government, meanwhile, made plans to distribute gas masks and began digging trenches in parks and gardens, including Buckingham Palace Gardens. "Keep calm and dig" was the slogan.

Churchill made his way back to the center of power. He reentered government in September, serving again as First Lord of the Admiralty, though now rather awkwardly under Chamberlain. "There are I believe a fair number of people who think and say that in these times Winston ought to be in the Government, but why?" asked the old diplomat Lord Hardinge. "Could anybody have a worse record? But we are a forgetful and forgiving people." In August, Churchill had gone to France to visit friends and the ex-wife of his cousin, the Duke of Marlborough. Before his return he remarked to an artist friend, "This is the last picture we shall paint in peace for a very long time."

Now a half-American buccaneer and a monarch with a list of German titles were again enlisted in saving the British Empire in a world war. The combination did not yet speak its name; neither man knew how much he would come to depend upon the other, if dependence is the right concept. This may be the biggest irony of all: in principle, neither a nation's savior nor its monarch needs a special ally. Each is supreme in his own role. Yet, as the next chapter will reveal, each is compromised. On the one hand, by the traditional British preference for mediocrity in its political class. It is a mediocrity that infects even the most exceptional of individuals, who must find a way to translate great virtue and power into a cause that is plausible and acceptable to the voting majority. And, on the other hand, by the tremendous demands placed upon him by a conflict so vast and so severe that no individual, however brilliant, can withstand them without the assistance and confidence of others. So a "mediocre" monarch joined an "exceptional" commoner in leading the nation during its finest hour. Before continuing the tale, there is more to say about the hearts and minds of both men.

CHAPTER SIX
Character

These were two very different and not naturally complementary personalities. Their relationship was asymmetrical. But then, how many great alliances are there between perfect equals? Among allies expediency usually outweighs parity. Political alliances especially are known to conflate apparent friendship—which always involves a certain degree of complementarity—with the ordering and intermingling of multiple interests, or, as Stalin once put it to Churchill, "The best friendships are those founded on misunderstandings." He might have said "mismatchings." Such asymmetries will be familiar to American readers because they occur regularly in our history, probably because of the combination of the roles of head of state and head of government in a single office. The partnership of Woodrow Wilson and Colonel House, Franklin Roosevelt and Harry Hopkins, Harry Truman and Dean Acheson, Richard Nixon and Henry Kissinger, and George W. Bush and Dick Cheney was that of a nominal superior and a subordinate—the latter an alter ego or, as was once said of Kissinger, an ego that was too big to alter.

Churchill's own associations with his secretary Edward Marsh and friends Brendan Bracken and Lords Birkenhead, Cherwell, and Beaverbrook have been much analyzed. Each could be said to have served a purpose beyond providing friendship: as political ambassadors, emissaries, confidants, and sounding boards. Other figures—the Americans Harry Hopkins, John Winant, and Averell Harriman, for example—would augment and insulate Churchill's position with Roosevelt. They are reminders that leaders—especially war leaders—perform collectively. In the case of Churchill, Roosevelt, and their respective chiefs of staff—Generals Alan Brooke and George Marshall—there was a "quartet of power," as Andrew Roberts has described it, that "danced [a] complicated minuet, each fearing the potentially disastrous consequences of getting out of step with the others." It did not perform in isolation; there were many others besides. Who were the real masters? The real commanders? Was the quartet really a prism, as Roberts has defined it? Or did it appear instead to thrive from a tension between opposites? Were they all opposites? And do opposites make for inherently stronger alliances—and leaders—than do more similar personalities? It may be better to think about them in a less mechanistic and more organic way: less as opposing or combining forces than as substances, having been treated for compatibility, mixing together in a solution.

Churchill, and to a lesser extent the king, surrounded himself with men who extended the zone of familiarity that was so important to him and who, to one degree or another, protected, charmed, and amused him. He shared intimacies frequently, but there was a certain imbalance to these friendships, since nearly all were devotees of Churchill as the central figure. There was Marsh, Churchill's loyal and long-suffering secretary during the early part of his career; Bracken, the brash Irish-Australian publicist, known as Churchill's "faithful chela"; Frederick Lindemann, "the Prof," later Lord Cherwell, a half-German, half–Anglo-American scientist known for his vegetarianism and related eccentricities. Earlier there had been the American financier Bernard Baruch; the Liberal politician F. E. Smith, later Lord Birkenhead; and the infamous, asthmatic Canadian press baron Max Aitken, Lord Beaverbrook—also known as the Beaver. Churchill's loyalty to these people was strong. One of his first acts after becoming prime minister was to propose Beaverbrook as minister of aircraft production and Bracken for the Privy Council. "What! Give him a peerage?" Churchill might have said mockingly about either man. "Well, perhaps, provided it's a disappearage." The king resisted both appointments, but Churchill would not give way.

Who were the king's close friends? There were his siblings—especially, until the abdication, David—and his cousin Louis "Dickie" Mountbatten. There was Louis Greig, the naval doctor and equerry who accompanied him to sea and sought to toughen him, and his private secretary Alan Lascelles. But there were few real friends, and it is tempting to ask whether an abundance of true friendships is rare or even possible for any monarch. This one in any event tended to prefer the company of acquaintances and servants, reserving nearly all his intimacies for his wife and daughters. To others he could seem dull, humorless, and awkward. "But," as Channon has written, "no one hated him—he was too neutral; hence he was a successful and even popular sovereign."

The position of a king toward his ministers is of a different but not unrelated character. Few monarchs arrive to their positions entirely on their own merits, and while some, as we have seen, may get there unexpectedly and after having passed a series of hard tests, the position almost always exists to be filled, not to be won, bought, seized, or concocted. Ministries are the opposite. They sit at the top of Benjamin Disraeli's greasy pole. While it is often the case that ministers are appointed for unusual reasons, prime ministers rarely are; the more successful ones, that is, the ones that tend to hold on to power by amassing it, almost never get there by chance. They tend to be ambitious, brutal, bloody-minded, versatile, nimble, malleable people. While that is all pretty obvious, less so is the quality of the interaction ministers must have with their monarchs. It is tricky, probably just as much as wooing electorates, defeating rivals, and mastering the difficult art of timing. Monarchs are fixed beings; they can only be removed with great difficulty; they generally demand deference and must not display weakness or passivity; they always require loyalty but also judgment and probably some degree of competence. One model for such an association was between Bismarck and Kaiser Wilhelm I. It worked well, though not always happily, for nearly three decades and produced, among other things, the modern German nation. Still, it was "hard to be Kaiser under Bismarck."

Most of today's constitutional monarchs are charity mavens and celebrities. This was not always true, even as recently as a generation ago. It was certainly not the case for prewar Britain. The British monarchy was an imperial one, and so carried different meanings to many subjects. Its apotheosis under Queen Victoria, like the empire itself, may have been impossible to perpetuate as it was. The special achievement of this king's father, George V, was to redefine so much of the loyalty to the monarchical and imperial idea for the twentieth century in the context of what would eventually be regarded as imperial decline by affixing to the institution an enduring affection for the royal family in public. Kings and queens, princes and princesses, and the rest had long been granted varying degrees of favor by the people, but in the twentieth century it came to be expressed more directly, maybe more intimately. For the first time their voices were heard on the radio and their faces seen in motion pictures, even on television.

The modern British monarchy was still something of a fragile flower, however. This is the main reason the abdication crisis carried so great a risk. It is difficult to name many chaste monarchs, but none—with the partial exception of George IV with Mrs. Fitzherbert, a precedent that Churchill once had the tactlessness to mention in Wallis Simpson's presence—had ever married his mistress, let alone a twice-married foreigner.

Devotion can be malleable. Thus Churchill's later about-face over the abdication may be explained as being consistent with his monarchism. It was said that "he venerated tradition, but ridiculed convention." Few would have challenged its sincerity. "No institution," he said, "pays such dividends as the Monarchy." His wife, Clementine, referred to him as "Monarchical No. 1." His was a form of devotion that placed a priority on institutions as well as legacies. "I was a child of the Victorian era," he had written in 1930, "when the structure of our country seemed firmly set, when its position in trade and on the seas was unrivalled, and when the realization of the greatness of our Empire and of our duty to preserve it was ever growing stronger." It was to be preserved, no matter the cost.

Yet there is a distinction between the institution and the person: "Dukes tended to believe they were as good as any monarch."

Respect and deference are not always dished out in equal measure. Churchill was said by his doctor, Lord Moran, to have a "positively regal" sense of himself, which was not necessarily inconsistent with his reverence for the actual monarchy. Perhaps, like his wartime railway coaches, Churchill's orientation was "semi-Royal," but this at times skated along the edges of irreverence. Edward VII once growled that his initials, W.C., were appropriate for the man. That king, like his son, eventually came around to giving Churchill something in the way of support, but never unconditional trust or affection. Other royals, such as George V's daughter-in-law, Elizabeth, had similar doubts about him. Lascelles could not bear him, and once even described him as "repugnant." Churchill returned the affection by calling him Alan instead of Tommy, which he preferred. This tendency to even the score occasionally hinted at republicanism, though never seriously. One of his first decisions at the Admiralty, for example, was to name a new battleship after Oliver Cromwell. (He later reversed the decision under pressure.) These are indications of his brand of humor: neither ribald nor dry, but playful, sometimes mocking. Another example came during the war, when an American bystander asked him the name of the "elephantine shuffle" the gruff, rotund Labour politician Ernest Bevin appeared to be doing on the dance floor. "What step was this, was it some old English step or dance?" The "P.M. looked, smiled and said, 'That's obviously the Labour movement.'"

Having presented on opposite sides of the abdication and appeasement questions, Churchill and the king might have been expected to get off to an uncomfortable start once Churchill reentered government. This did not happen for three reasons. The king may have been the alternative to and beneficiary of his brother's disgrace, but in fact he and Churchill were on the same side in that instance, at least in principle and in public, especially regarding the position of Wallis Simpson. The king's real views on the appeasement policy are harder to pin down. More than anything else he seemed concerned, perhaps bemused, by it. Again, he, like many people in Britain, was desperate to forgo entering another war. Which of course is not the same thing as saying they were tolerant, let alone backers, of Nazi tyranny. Finally, it is important to remember that neither man was unknown to the other: there was a history of contact, albeit not familiarity, going back decades.

The two would settle into their new roles without a clean slate. It may have been tarnished, but it was strengthened by shared expectations. For the king this meant above all the right to be consulted, the right to encourage, and the right to warn. The triple formula had come from Walter Bagehot, whose classic interpretation of the place of royalty in the country's constitution emphasized the distinction between official and personal devotion, with the moral representation of the royal family paramount. The new king grasped the point. He had studied Bagehot, and was already known for having a strong sense of duty. Robert Rhodes James has added two other important qualities: ability and luck. Both may be tempered, diminished or enhanced, as the case may be, by the nature of relations between a monarch and his or her ministers. In Rhodes James's account, the modern British monarchy evolved during the course of the nineteenth century from one having a confrontational to a cooperative role with governments. This was a way of enhancing, maybe refining, ability and mitigating the effects of bad luck.

The next subject is bravery. The king's bravery, unlike Churchill's, was compensatory, since he was not naturally fearless. His had to be cultivated. They shared this "supreme quality," the one Churchill had said, "which guarantees all others." Churchill once recalled the encounter he had in the First World War with General John French, in which French said that he did not worry about being shot while "look[ing] over the parapet." If he lived, he would adjust his life accordingly. Performing such a risky act on purpose was another matter. Risk for risk's sake did not bring the same dividends. The primary measure of bravery, then, was less inherent than circumstantial. But you had to take risks, especially if you were born with the ability to avoid them. Choosing to "not mingle in the hurly-burly" did not gain a person credit in Churchill's book.

What of other qualities: Affection? Charity? These fall under the rubric of friendship. It is a different concept. Lord Birkenhead, among others, has said of Churchill, "He has never in all his life failed a friend, however embarrassing the obligation which he felt it was necessary to honour." Churchill revered some elements of friendship over others, chief among which was the pleasantness of another's company, its "rich and positive quality," as he put it. Birkenhead had this quality in abundance. He made Churchill happy.

Both the king and Churchill, however, had few real friends, or at least few who could be considered equals. They were essentially friendless. How, then, to explain their own friendship? Churchill was devoted to the king and the king came to be in awe of Churchill, and the latter may be the more significant historical fact, for it tended to deepen whatever initial devotion the minister may have felt toward his monarch. This in turn speaks to the power of their particular asymmetry. Britain breeds loads of dutiful, worthy, upright, and not very intelligent people, and the king was clearly one of them. He was neither clever nor cunning. He presented the best virtues of that British invention: the "moderate and politically uninterested London clubman," whose gentlemanly ideal was one of "temperance, magnificence, good-temper, justice and a certain kindliness." Mental ability and temperament are not always matched consistently. The latter, as the familiar line about Roosevelt goes—a man with a second-class intellect but a first-class temperament—can count for a great deal in a leader.

Prime ministers are generally afraid of worrying their monarchs because assuaging their fears can be time-consuming, and because having an upset monarch on one's hands is just unpleasant, and possibly risky. In this case, the king was a born worrier, and even more so when he saw what Churchill was dealing with in the war. Churchill by contrast was not a worrier but a "despairer": "Worry is a spasm of the emotion; the mind catches hold of something and will not let it go," he wrote. Hence one explanation for his attention to the king. Sharing his worries may have reduced the chances of despair taking hold. The king was perpetually anxious and knew he did not know how to handle many things. Unlike his father, for example, he kept his fingers out of party politics and most questions of policy. Churchill may have occasionally regarded him like a pet, knowing that the king felt he was dealing with a superman who was clearly out of the king's class and whose decisions he almost always accepted, even when he disagreed. This was not true the other way around. Ziegler has put the point more succinctly: "He would have died for the cause of the King if this had seemed necessary, but it would not have occurred to him to alter a detail of his budget or to shuffle the members of a ministry because he believed that to be the King's desire." It is tempting, then, but not entirely accurate, to call this patronizing.

Churchill extended to the king the reassurance that he needed in order to reassure the British people. The king understood and respected him for it. The result was good. Asymmetry can work two ways. It was once said of the relationship between Halifax and Churchill that they "are a very good combination as they act as a stimulus and brake on each other." It could just as well have applied here.

Asymmetry, therefore, was one source of the alliance's strength. A more symmetrical match might have meant a dangerous clash of wills. Asymmetry, however, is not always conducive to subordination. This is apparent from Churchill's complex and often difficult wartime relations with his military commanders and political allies.

Franklin Roosevelt performed his own role as commander in chief with detachment; he deferred nearly all operational decisions to General Marshall and the secretary of war, Henry Stimson. Stalin commanded, it is presumed, with a heavier hand. Only Churchill had the burden (some would say advantage) of a constant battle of wits against his senior commanders, who challenged his judgment as often as he belittled theirs. It was not war command by seminar, but it was hardly smooth, simple, or uniformly effective. Churchill took his combined ministerial role seriously, perhaps too seriously. His commanders generally praised his performance as prime minister. He held the country together, gave it hope, strengthened its resolve, and tended its alliances as well as nearly anyone else could have done. His performance as head of the Defence Ministry was another matter. And as a commander who "adored funny operations," he was said to be dismal.

He drove some serving under him to distraction. One put it this way: "If he were a woman I could put up with him. If he were an Elizabeth I or Cleopatra. But Gloriana with a cigar I cannot stomach." Churchill recognized the problem but cast it in a positive light. "They may say I lead them up the garden path," he said of his chiefs, "but at every turn of the path they have found delectable fruits and wholesome vegetables." He pushed hard, but he did so not for its own sake but to get better results, which he often got.

It is a commonplace but bears repeating: as wartime leader he was certainly dictatorial but he was no dictator. Once, he told the king "that his fellow Ministers spent all their time telling him he was wrong and that such a project could not be carried out. 'Perhaps they're sometimes right,' said the king, with a smile. 'Nine times out of ten,' replied Mr. Churchill, unabashed." But these were methods, not aims. Fighting a war was not the same as winning a debate, a charge the Labour politician Aneurin Bevan once leveled against him. He did not insist on his way no matter what, not all the time. His goal was not the permanent state of his own power, however indispensable he may have believed it was. Nor was it to win arguments for their own sake. His goal was victory for his country. Thus, despite the fury that he provoked in a few of those who served under him, there was less of a split between the politicians and the generals than there had been during the previous war.

Some, like John Dill, the chief of the Imperial General Staff (CIGS)—Britain's senior military commander—had so much trouble working with Churchill (who liked to call him "Dilly Dally") that he just appeared to surrender. Alas, Dill would not survive the war, which has led to the charge that Churchill "killed men who could not keep up . . . just as Napoleon Bonaparte killed horses under him." Dill in the end was better suited to what would become his last assignment, to Washington, where he mastered a partnership with Marshall that was second only in importance to the one Churchill had developed with Roosevelt. It was that important, not only because of the deep differences between Churchill and Marshall and the other generals over strategy, but also because it was believed by some that Dill's replacement as CIGS, Alan Brooke, had trouble working with Americans, including—partially—Churchill.

Where Marshall appreciated Dill's thoughtful, rational nature, Churchill was dismissive. In consequence, Dill "would often relapse into tongue-tied silence" or complain, as Admiral John Fisher, Churchill's longtime nemesis from the navy, once did, "He out-argues me." Relations between the two were beset as much by bad chemistry as by bad luck. There was the time, for example, when they went to see a demonstration of a weapon, a kind of missile designed to seek and destroy tanks. One misfired and headed straight for Dill; another went after Churchill. He ran as fast as he could and missed being hit when the rocket landed nearby. "Damn the man!" he shouted. "I won't speak to him for a week."

Dill went on to perform yeoman's service in America, as would Halifax as ambassador. Who would have guessed, in Halifax's case, that "a great aristocrat, noted as a Master of Foxhounds, who in his political career had been closely identified with the policy of Munich, and to whom the American continent was *terra incognita*" would prove such an inspired choice? Not those who saw a man who, shortly after arriving in America, asked an embassy attaché, "What shall I say to them? I've never seen so many mayors in my life." The attaché replied, "Quite easy. Just whinny like a stallion."

Another who suffered from Churchill's impatience was Archibald Wavell, the general who headed the Middle East Command. He was said to be "the luckiest general in the war." Churchill supposedly regarded him as " 'a good average colonel' who would make a 'good chairman of a Tory association.' " A " 'still waters running deep' sort of man," Wavell could be laconic to an extreme. His silence even disturbed the king. "Why does Winston dislike me?" Wavell asked. Churchill never gave the reason. Being inarticulate had something to do with it. Halifax had a better answer: Churchill "hates doormats. If you begin to give way he will simply wipe his feet upon you." Like Halifax and Dill, Wavell would be packed off— in his case, to India.

Others familiar to students of the war included Claude Auchinleck, "the Auk," who was the man on the other side from Wavell on Churchill's two fishing rods when he said, "I feel that I have got a tired fish on this rod, and a very lively one on the other." Replacing Wavell as commander in the Middle East in the summer of 1941, Auchinleck was a charmer to whom Churchill remained too loyal for too long. He felt similarly, perhaps even more so, toward Harold Alexander, who replaced Auchinleck in the Middle East and then went on to command the Allied armies in Italy. Alexander was probably his favorite commander, although his achievements on the ground were sometimes lacking. With another prima donna, Bernard Montgomery, the issuing of praise was more complicated. Churchill tolerated but did not enjoy Monty. There was a certain clash of egos, not to mention the occasional flare of jealousy. Churchill once asked Brooke,

"Why did not the king give Monty his [field marshal's] baton when he visited him in France?"

"[P]robably one was not ready."

"No! . . . [T]hat's not it. Monty wants to fill the Mall when he gets his baton! And he will not fill the Mall!" . . .

[T]here was no reason for Monty to fill the Mall on that occasion. But he continued, "Yes, he will fill the Mall because he is Monty, and I will not have him filling the Mall!"

Churchill's tendency, when unhappy with a commander's progress, was to drown him in memoranda. Hastings Ismay, Churchill's principal military aide and secretary of the Committee of Imperial Defence, urged a commander not "to be irritated by these never-ending messages, but to remember that Churchill, as Prime Minister and Minister of Defence, bore the primary responsibility for ensuring that all available resources . . . were apportioned . . . in the best interests of the war effort as a whole."

Ismay, known as Pug, was an exception: if he got exasperated, he rarely showed it. He was a tall, solid cavalryman who had once been a polo champion:

Characteristic of straightforward and practical common-sense were his round head and square capable hands, the other side of his nature being compound in his large brilliant eyes [that] mirrored a clairvoyant foresight, a psychic perception of men's foibles and, more often than not, a sure discernment of their true motives. They also made him a formidable cardplayer who knew the whereabouts of any card in the pack.

Ismay's role was to be the greaser of wheels and the impartial arbiter. It required diplomatic skill. But Ismay could take a stand when one was necessary. Once when Churchill asked him what he really thought about a certain question, the answer was definite: "Do you wish me to be of value to you or not?" "Naturally..." "Then ... you will never ask me that question again."

Churchill's relations were more strained with the man who became the most important military commander to serve him: Brooke, who replaced Dill as CIGS. Brooke was a strict, stern, dark, and dour Anglo-Irish soldier whose family had served in the army for generations. He was Britain's top general in more than one respect: Ismay regarded him as simply the "best" of the eight chiefs of the Imperial General Staff he had known.

Having grown up in France, Brooke knew Europe as well as any of his counterparts. Like Churchill, he could be impatient—he "thought fast, talked fast, moved fast"—but unlike him, he bore grudges. "Brookie," however, could stomach Churchill far better than Dill. His biographer and onetime editor of his diaries, Arthur Bryant, has described him as Churchill's unrecognized "complement" who matched the man's inspiration with the ability to perceive practicalities—and impracticalities—at all levels. The two argued over them endlessly. To his credit, Churchill took part in these arguments and allowed himself to be challenged; the only alternative would have been to dismiss Brooke, which he could have done but never did. Seeing him as an equal, or even in possession of a superior military mind, cut deeply against Churchill's grain, not only because he had been a professional soldier himself and a self-assured one at that, but also because of the experience of the last war, when the commanders had failed their country so badly. It had a lasting effect on him and on practically every other politician of his generation. Where the king's instinct toward the military professionals was for deference, with Churchill it was the opposite, which they in turn must have wanted to reciprocate. Thus what Churchill must have sought from his commanders was not inspiration or passion but order, or to counter the tendency, as he liked to say, to "devot[e] more time to self-expression than to self-discipline." He had the sense to know it, in Brooke's case, eventually.

It has been said that Churchill and Brooke represented the opposing minds of the artist and the scientist. There is some truth to this. For if Brooke understood anything, it was the calibration and the concentration of power. He was first and foremost an artilleryman. Brooke loved the artillery. He thought and wrote about it his entire life. This not only inspired an obsession with firepower that would come in useful during the war, but also an important preoccupation with careful planning as well as a faith in the ultimate value of attrition, despite the suffering it had brought during the previous war. That this time attrition came from the air rather than from the trenches seemed not to alter the basic concept. This was in marked contrast to Churchill's antiquated fixation upon maneuver and mobility. "Why should the New Armies be sent to 'chew barbed wire'?" His brief time in the trenches during the last war only confirmed the view. He simply hated immobility, which he equated with inaction and potential slaughter, not prudence and preparation. Churchill railed against "mountains of impedimenta." "[S]haking his fist in the CIGS' face, he said, 'I do not want any of your own long term projects. . . . All they do is cripple initiative.'" Brooke later exclaimed, "I feel like a man chained to the chariot of a lunatic!!"

This is another way of saying that Brooke was incorrect in claiming that he and the generals had strategy while Churchill merely had guesswork. There was more to the contrast, which in the event had mostly to do with a struggle for complementarity. And the extent to which Brooke imparted these views to the king—the above quotations appear on the same page of Brooke's diary as a visit to Buckingham Palace, for example—cannot be known, though they probably counted. Nevertheless, to Brooke, Churchill was the essential, if impossible, man: "God knows where we would be without him, but God knows where we shall go with him!"

Tenacity was one reason why Churchill was so successful a war leader. "Whatever the P.M.'s shortcomings may be, there is no doubt that he does provide guidance and purpose for the Chiefs of Staff and the [Foreign Office] on matters which, without him, would often be lost in the maze of inter-departmentalism or frittered away by caution and compromise." He fought constantly against what he had earlier praised as the "common Staff brain."

For Churchill really did understand mobile warfare; he had, after all, been one of the first to invest in experimental "landships" (tanks) and was regarded as a leading "apostle of the offensive." Yet he also understood, or thought he understood, what Brooke knew in spades: the vital role of firepower. He may not have really understood the progress in mechanization that armies had made since the last war, and almost certainly never understood the effective management of supply lines. "When I was a soldier," he said, "infantry used to walk and cavalry used to ride. But now the infantry require motor-cars." There was obviously much more to modern warfare. This is the reason why he needed the constructive opposition of Brooke, and vice versa.

No military commander welcomes the meddling and second-guessing of politicians, least of all one as intellectually powerful and bloody-minded as Churchill. Brooke has drawn a contrast with the dealings of Marshall and Roosevelt in which the latter "listened" and more or less took whatever "advice" the former gave him. This was not likely to have been the case for Stalin, however, who, according to Brooke, "had a military brain of the very highest calibre." With Churchill it was not always clear where one stood. "When I thump the table and push my face towards him what does he do? Thumps the table harder and glares back at me. . . . I know these Brookes—stiff-necked Ulstermen and there's no one worse to deal with than that!" Perhaps neither man could make up his mind about the military brain. "How often have I seen Winston eyeing me carefully trying to read my innermost thoughts," Brooke noted, "searching for any doubts that might rest under the surface."

There were indeed times when the relationship seemed near collapse, but there is also evidence that Churchill fought the impulse to quit. When asked if he could ever reach the point of dismissing Brooke, Churchill said, "Never," then again, after "a long pause, 'Never.'" But just a few weeks after being appointed CIGS, Brooke wondered if he should resign in favor of another person who could better handle Churchill. Ismay reported this to Churchill, who said, "General Brooke—resign? Why no—I'm very fond of him, and I need him!" Even so, "Brooke was the only man on whom" Churchill was later seen to "deliberately and ostentatiously turn his back." On yet another occasion Churchill blurted out, "Brooke must go! I cannot work with him. He hates me. I can see hatred looking from his eyes!" When Ismay told this to Brooke, the general replied, "Hate him? I don't hate him. I *love* him. But the first time I tell him I agree with him when I don't will be the time to get rid of me, for then I will be of no more use to him." Ismay reported back, "The

CIGS says he doesn't hate you. He loves you! But if he ever tells you he agrees when he doesn't you must get rid of him as no more use." Churchill, whose eyes were said to fill with tears, said only, "*Dear Brooke!*" The general later concluded, "You left him with the feeling that you would do anything within your power to help him carry the stupendous burden he had shouldered."

Churchill's relations with Brooke contrasted with others, notably admirals and air marshals, with whom he spent less time. One reason was that none had the same stature or ability. Much of what has been written about Admiral Dudley Pound, for example, was of how often he slept. Churchill was said to be fonder of Admiral Andrew Cunningham, who did not reciprocate, reportedly viewing Churchill as a cavalryman out of his depth on naval matters. He was even fonder of Air Marshal Charles Portal, but he has written less about him than he has about army generals. This was strange given Churchill's deep interest in both the Admiralty and the Royal Air Force. His more strenuous military associations tended to be the more important ones, which provide a comparison to his alliance with the king: stature alone did not suffice, nor did a degree of mutual affection. There was also the mental contest.

A similar pattern was evident with regard to political allies. Churchill had some positive feeling for Anthony Eden, the man he meant to succeed him, but within limits, as Eden's own frequent bouts of exasperation during the war—Churchill called them attacks of "Foreign-officissimus"—attest. The king was reported to think less of Eden but deferred to Churchill. Had both he and Eden somehow been killed, Churchill's nominee for successor was John Anderson, the economic war coordinator and chancellor of the exchequer (and overseer of Britain's atomic warfare research), but a man toward whom Churchill felt no intimacy whatever, apart from the indirect association there was with his late friend Ralph Wigram, whose widow Anderson had married.

Toward his private secretaries and other civilian aides he was mainly paternalistic, sometimes intolerable, and often generous. He could be devastating toward them; other times he could be kind and jocular. Typists were especially hard put. Churchill could be difficult to follow when they took dictation, and he was merciless with errors. But every now and then he let a mistake go without a tantrum, as when a secretary typed "lemons" instead of "Lemnos." His aides deserve brief mention if only because a few, like Joan Astley and John "Jock" Colville, have left behind such vivid portraits.

Finally something more must be said about the men's families. The importance of the king's devotion to the queen and the princesses, and Churchill's to his wife, Clemmie, has already been noted. Churchill adored his daughters, especially Mary and Sarah. However, relations with his son, Randolph, a drunkard and boaster, became bitter. Churchill was said to be afraid of him because he was so unmanageable. Toward his sons-in-law, he could be occasionally doting but never entrusted any of them, with the partial exception of Christopher Soames, with the clear expectation of succession, much unlike the role he assumed for himself vis-à-vis his own father. The king was more fortunate in his progeny. He adored his daughters and was especially close to the eldest, Lilibet, who was most like him, though her shyness, like his, mellowed with age. While she may have been "good at trying to find words for strangers . . . it is a great strain for her. Not so for Princess Margaret Rose who burbles away naturally and easily."

How much did various personal and private relations affect the war? It is impossible to qualify them without returning to the concept of adversity. Lord Moran has said that the "English rather like a man who hasn't come off, anyway if he is staunch and uncomplaining in adversity." He applied the trait to Churchill:

> [I]t's a man's character that counts with us, not his achievements. . . . Winston seems to me to be a hundred per cent American in his feelings about failure. Unless a man has done something in life, something really worth doing, he does not interest Winston. The fact that he has not come off and is a bit of a failure merely depresses him. It is what a man does, not what he is, that counts.

At root Churchill was probably deeply afraid of failure. Moran continued, "[W]hen the sun shines his arrogance, intolerance and cocksureness assume alarming proportions." But "[i]n adversity Winston becomes gentle, patient and brave." He "grows in" it. Failure and adversity made each man stronger by distilling his character. To Moran adversity was "first cousin" to Churchill's "pugnacity." In the king it was a constant companion that sifted and sorted and reduced him to his fundamental nature. When faced with the prospect, or the consequences, of adversity or failure, most people do not triumph over them right away; first they must toss overboard all the excess baggage of character, the traits that have been acquired and honed self-consciously over the years in the luxury of happier circumstances and as representations of the people they would otherwise like to be. Real adversity forces them to face who they really are. It forces them to confront the extent of their strength and weakness. In so doing, it extends and sharpens the capacity for empathy. Knowing themselves that much more allows them to know others better, and vice versa.

Adversity has an either/or quality: it kills or it builds strength; it defeats or is overcome; it blesses by its absence or curses by its presence in people's lives. It is, however, more reciprocal and cumulative with its function than absolute or final. It is at once a burden and a test, therefore, less than it is so much one or the other. It has every ability to destroy but not necessarily to defeat—to borrow a distinction from Hemingway—and there are many shades in between. The effects of adversity rest in the strength and nature of the character that meets it, however much that character is shaped by it in response.

That is how it works in practice. The effort and the quality of a role were at one with its effects. Of Churchill's three classes of people—"those who are toiled to death, those who are worried to death, and those who are bored to death"—he and the king were determined to spare each other the fate of the first two, while the final seemed irrelevant. Both men tried hard, though not everyone else grasped the roles they played. It was said, for example, that the reason Rudolf Hess made his famous landing on the estate of the Duke of Hamilton was because Hess understood that the duke was the Lord Steward, and so may have thought the duke would be the perfect person to persuade the king to make a separate peace. "This greatly amused Churchill. . . . 'I suppose he thinks the Duke carves the chicken and consults the King as to whether he likes breast or leg!'" In reality there was very little the Duke of Hamilton could do for Hess. The king found his persuasion elsewhere.

Of the many clichés that fill the biographical literature about the king, probably the two most tiresome refer to his need to gain self-confidence and to the favorable impression he made on first-time acquaintances. Churchill also defied certain stereotypes. There can be no doubt that he was a great man, but not "in the way Lloyd George was; but undeniably a great personality, which is another matter." Put differently, as he liked to say, "I am arrogant, but not conceited." Others would say that "[h]e has genius without judgment." And there is Baldwin's familiar quip:

> [W]hen Winston was born lots of fairies swooped down on his cradle bearing gifts—imagination, eloquence, industry, ability, and then came a fairy who said "No one person has a right to so many gifts," picked him up and gave him such a shake and a twist that with all these gifts he was denied judgement and wisdom.

So he was talented, indeed, but not, in the end, superhuman. He understood the value of subtlety, and was not so patently the belli-cose, juvenile, exhibitionistic, uncooperative figure of popular insult. Yet just as the various presumptions about the king's character had some basis in fact, so did those about Churchill.

Where did they come from? Churchill's mind was "a powerful machine," in the words of Lloyd George, "but there lay hidden in its material or make-up some obscure defect which prevented it from always running true." The real defect was authority. There was something just slightly too unusual with Churchill; the superiority of his talent was, in the British setting, almost exotic. His tie to the king served to ground him, to temper his nature, or at least to diminish his tendency to incapacitate those around him. Their alliance, then, was about refining and selling each other's character as much as it was about duty and prerogative, or about clarifying each other's thinking. Churchill's propensity to immerse himself in the tiniest details has been noted often, yet less understood perhaps is the critical role his regular meetings with the king played in helping him to settle, clarify, and order the many details in the form of a familiar tutorial or briefing. Churchill liked variety but not unfamiliarity. He had trouble with strangers or opponents and resisted them. With such people he "sidles away from one . . . looks down as he talks," and "seems to contract, suddenly to look smaller and his famous charm is overclouded by an angry taurine look." If demanding endless details from his subordinates was a means for expending great energy, then releasing it through recitation in the presence of the king must have performed a similar function within the familiar bounds of official duty. Doing so helped each man conquer long-standing and debilitating defects in his character, not least of which was a depressive tendency that was kept well hidden. Each man when with the other was seen to some degree as working against his own faults on behalf of the other. If true, it would go a long way toward explaining how they could strip their personal relationship down to the bare essentials in order to rebuild it with an armature of knowledge and trust. That was their mutual invention. It and the partnerships discussed above served a critical purpose for each man that spread in turn by way of their cumulative enhancement of a combined character. They, as was said about Churchill, did not "tilt at windmills . . . [or] embrace lost causes, but sought rather the very roots and sources of power, gauging with sure insight the hidden springs." This showed that adversity's silver lining must be polished constantly and reciprocally "till it shone after its fashion." Nobody can be whole on his own.

That was the special role of each man for the other. For Britain already had a permanent ruler with a role to perform. The evidence suggests that most of their Tuesday "picnics"—their weekly lunches, which began in September 1940—were filled with discussions of operations, the kind of talk the king craved. Mastering the brief brought satisfaction. Churchill's self-confidence in facts and presentation must have rubbed off. The exchange may have served an additional purpose in forcing their individual and collective minds to set the best priorities possible, as an obsession with details may do for some people who use it to tame the imagination, adjust perspective, and prevent panic over complexity.

Without having been present in the room, it is difficult to say for certain precisely how Churchill and the king underwent such a process together. The king said that the meetings were the "high points of the week." As for Churchill, according to Rhodes James,

> What particularly impressed him about the King was the latter's total application to his job in every respect, not least in his careful and thorough reading of all documents put before him. Also, as matters progressed, and the King and Queen travelled throughout the country—far more than Churchill or his principal ministers could—they were in a better position than most to assess the public mood.

The effect of their meetings and its significance to history exist only in outline, despite all that has been written about each man. Yet the outline is suggestive and significant. The two dined alone, or sometimes with the queen, who, for all intents and purposes, was one with the king so far as knowing his character, apart from her pleasant exterior disguising a "small drop of arsenic in the centre of that marshmallow." When the king was away, she met Churchill in his stead. The king and the prime minister served themselves at table, as there were almost never any servants present. Churchill was called a "selective listener." The king was a selective talker. For all that Churchill liked to be the source of his own information and for all that the king did not like to volunteer it, this is probably what took place between them, and sometimes in reverse, resulting in a form of multidimensional asymmetry, if such a thing can exist. For Churchill, at least, "[n]o subject had ever been so honoured. He wanted no other reward."

To analyze the full function of the debates happening on both sides of Churchill—above with his monarch and below with his commanders—would seem to require the training of a Gestalt psychologist. They operated as something more than a double-sided sounding board. The ideas, feelings, judgments, and facts did not merely bounce back at Churchill so as to allow confirmation or the occasional refutation of his decisions. Indeed, they may have served a more subtle purpose, which had more to do, again, with the essence of his leadership than with its exercise. They reinforced his position of authority, and his mission, as servant of the state by reminding him of the fundamental necessity of leading a consensus. Some of Churchill's candor—in language and sentiment, especially—could taste sour in the mouths of his enemies. Yet candor and clarity did not come easily to him. He worked at them. His initial thoughts were often muddled and indiscriminate. He distilled and polished them, oftentimes out loud, until he felt they were at their best and purest. Like most literary brains, Churchill's needed a dedicated editor. In his own way, which could sometimes seem perverse and self-defeating, Churchill sought and encouraged the tough resistance of those around him, not merely to enhance his own character or position (although this was often a by-product) but to get better results. Remove any of the elements—Parliament, the press, the chiefs, or the king—and the machine was flawed, even doomed. Churchill was as much its cog as its engineer.

CHAPTER SEVEN
Personality

I t is an error to regard the imagination as a mainly revolutionary force," Isaiah Berlin has written. "[I]f it destroys and alters,
it also fuses hitherto isolated beliefs, insights, mental habits,
into strongly unified systems. These, if they are filled with sufficient energy and force of will . . . sometimes transform the out-
look of an entire people and generation." This is another key to
understanding the king's contribution to Churchill—a buoy or
mast to which he fastened his imagination.

Churchill could be unpredictable and inconsiderate, but he was
rarely obtuse. His approach to life was zestful, extreme. Hence his
combination of optimism and hope with intense bouts of depression, and an outer shell of complexity over what some people
regarded as a rather simple, straightforward soul. Churchill was
clumsy when he tried to deceive, and he almost never did. He was
almost pathologically transparent.

He could be dismissive, even forgetful, but rarely absent-
minded. His inadvertencies appeared deliberate. During the war,
for example, he liked to forget (or pretend to forget) codes, as in a

phone call with Eden during which Eden, "[s]peaking slowly and carefully," said, "I went to the ironmonger's and there I bought—" to which Churchill replied, "*What? . . . What* are you talking about? I thought you had been to see the Turks!" Or when he reported to Roosevelt that he was coming to Washington by top secret "puff puff." Sometimes on the telephone he would pretend to be his secretary John Martin, thereby causing the latter much trouble with the censors.

Churchill was, then, a believer in both chance and the permanence of character, and to understand how that operated vis-à-vis the king, something more must be said of habits and customs.

It was not simply the fact that Churchill, like many great men, was a bundle of contradictions or that the contradictions had contradictions, but that they blurred so often with convictions, as in Lady Lytton's familiar line: "[T]he first time you meet Winston you see all his faults, and the rest of your life you spend in discovering his virtues." The latter may have been ends justifying the former. Or that it just took longer for Churchill's underlying faith to be revealed from the fog of his adversarial temperament, "so adjacent that he comes a damn sight near to being contiguous."

This adjacent aspect also governed his approach to history and his tendency, at times, to conflate its breadth and its depth. "Winston," his wife once said, "has always seen things in blinkers." It was appropriate that in his study at Chequers, his country residence, Churchill kept two objects: a large globe given to him by General Marshall, and an epidiascope, which was a device used to view small objects on reconnaissance photographs. His historical imagination was so rich it tended to smother all present and future realities within a powerful, even mythical, past. This led now and again to a failure to place short-term problems in their proper context, and to rely instead on the luck of the draw when events did not conform to the larger plan or, as he put it, to "take refuge beneath the impenetrable arch of probability." This way of thinking went against that of the king, who clung to habits, certainties, and rituals.

There were some more apparent, and some less apparent, qualities they had in common. The more apparent were the physical ones: Both were fair, even pale, as young men. Both had smooth skin and, in Churchill's case, unusually small, delicate hands, which he kept so well that they looked idle. These refinements contrasted with the gait familiar to most people—the hunched shoulders and glaring expression, which also remolded itself every now and then into a sly grin.

For someone so theatrical, Churchill was remarkably free of physical vanity. Legend holds that he verged on the exhibitionistic. There is the oft-repeated story of his accidental encounter in the nude with Roosevelt in the White House when he said that the British prime minister has nothing to hide from the American president. Since he spent so much time working in bed, it was not unusual for assistants to find him coming out of the bath or in various states of undress. Even when traveling, he customarily slept in nothing but one of his special silk underclothes; once, seven thousand feet in the air when he awoke from the cold, he tried to fasten a blanket to the side of the plane to keep out a draft. "On his hands and knees," Lord Moran has recalled, he "cut a quaint figure with his big, bare, white bottom."

Both Churchill and the king had been small boys who compensated for physical disadvantage with courage. Churchill's physical courage, or as some have said, rashness, showed early. He once fell from a tree and perforated a kidney; on a holiday visit to Lausanne he nearly drowned in the lake and came closest in this instance, he said, to staring death in the face. Later, after being hit by a car in New York, he took weeks to recover from his injuries.

The king had written a note to himself: "The schoolboy's definition of courage: That part of you which says 'stick it' while the rest of you says 'chuck it.'" While Churchill was of a fundamentally strong physical constitution, and the king of a much weaker one, both had confronted illness with fortitude. Both were athletic. The king had excellent hand-eye coordination, and so was a superb rider, tennis player, and pilot; Churchill, even as an old man, impressed onlookers by his agility, telling a young naval officer who offered his hand, for example, "Young man, do you suppose I have never climbed a ladder in my life?" One day at Buckingham Palace, he was pointed to the lift. "'Lift?' demanded the indignant prime minister. He ran up the stairs two at a time, then turned and thumbed his nose at the courtier." He liked to dart up hills or around fortifications like an agile crab. "On one such occasion," Colville has related, "he leapt off the top of a high girder into a pool of liquid cement. His feet were embedded."

"That is your Waterloo," Colville said.

"Blenheim . . . how dare you! I am not a Frenchman."

Colville concluded: "[A]fter two gruelling years of endless work and never a day's holiday, he was gay, resilient and apparently tireless. . . . Extraordinary in a man of almost sixty-six who never takes exercise of any sort."

Churchill's tough constitution occasionally succumbed to strain, and he was not always as limber or as lucky as he might have liked to think. He compensated by being droll. Once, when inspecting a kind of antiaircraft device, its wires crossed and it exploded directly above him. He said, without removing the cigar from his mouth, "I think there is something not quite right about the way you are using this new weapon."

He sometimes reacted badly to the strain of overconcentration. The solution, which he arrived at during his time as Home Secretary, was to make lists. On these he would organize his problems into categories from the least to the greatest, and then focus mainly on the latter. Perhaps this was another feature of his weekly meetings with the king.

His illnesses and injuries were rarely light. He was not the best of patients and challenged the expertise of doctors with his own theories or rationales, such as relying on the king's advice for malaria medication, for example, over the orders of medical professionals. Or he would self-medicate, taking snuff, for example, to cure a cold; consulting a variety of doctors until he got the opinion he wanted; or simply sorting his cure from the leftover medicines he already had. It was not surprising that his doctor, Lord Moran, penned so unflattering, if affectionate, a portrait of him. Their introduction in May 1940 more or less set the pattern:

> I have become his doctor, not because he wanted one, but because certain members of his Cabinet . . . have decided somebody ought to keep an eye on his health. . . .
>
> "I don't know why they are making such a fuss. There's nothing wrong with me. . . . I suffer from dyspepsia, and this is the treatment."
>
> With that he proceeded to demonstrate to me some breathing exercises. His big white belly was moving up and

down. . . . Soon after I took my leave. I do not like the job, and
I do not think the arrangement can last.

It lasted another quarter of a century, until Churchill's death,
through one "heart attack . . . three attacks of pneumonia . . . two
strokes . . . two operations . . . senile pruritis . . . conjunctivitis," and
numerous other smaller maladies. Many of these problems—
including the heart attack and the pneumonia—took place during
the war.

The king worried after Churchill's health, writing to him often
to "beg of you to take care of yourself & get as much rest as you possibly can in these critical days," as did others, including Roosevelt,
Brooke, and Eden. "If you go on playing the fool like this," Bracken
told him, "you are certain to die." Ismay recalled, "That kept him
quiet, but not for long." The strain was felt by many of those around
him: colleagues and secretaries forced to keep his hours, and particularly members of his household staff. The small, bald, lisping,
and devoted valet, Sawyers, bore the brunt, though he, too, occasionally invited rebuke, as when he once placed a dab of shoe polish
on Churchill's toothbrush and handed it to him. Brooke recalled
another episode when Churchill addressed him with the usual
rudeness: "'What's wrong, Sawyers? Why are you getting in my
way?' In a very thick voice Sawyers replied: 'The brim of your hat is
turned up, does not look well, turn it down, turn it down!' This was
accompanied by a waving gesture of the hand. Winston, rather red
and looking angry, turned the brim down. Thereupon Sawyers
stood to one side, muttering to himself 'That's much, much better,
much better.'"

Churchill's tendency to seek rejuvenation of the spirit should be seen in connection with similar efforts, however faulty, to rejuvenate the body. He fought often against his black moods but could be remarkably resilient. Once, during the war, he was visited in bed by Beaverbrook.

> He felt ill [and] said to Max: "I'm through. I cannot carry the burdens any longer." The second front was worrying him and he was right down. He said: "I have done my job. The Americans are in and we cannot lose. Anthony can carry on. I must get out." While this depression was at its height, the white telephone by his bed rang loudly. The government had been defeated in the House of Commons. Winston threw off the bedclothes, hurled himself out of bed with a glint of battle in his eye, said to Max: "I need a life of action!"

Churchill and the king both thought and spoke poorly on their feet, or at least they thought they did, although the king reckoned he was better at speaking extemporaneously than he was at reading aloud. Both men had overcome speech defects—Churchill earlier than the king—although the former admitted some time later that only the war had finally cured him of the anxiety he felt before giving a speech. He had the additional early disadvantage of having his talents contrasted unfavorably with the eloquent and clear voice of his father.

Churchill was principally a writer more than he was a speaker and so made careful preparation and skillful borrowing a habit. He became so good at writing by dictation that he could claim that he "lived from mouth to hand" and that "he wrote his speeches and spoke his books." The latter were dictated, a practice that had begun at Harrow with a friend who would take down what young Winston said.

Several who worked with Churchill commented upon the method, resembling percolation, by which he found and memorized the perfect word or phrase. He would either hear it or think it, repeat it a few times, play it over and again in his mind while listening to Gilbert and Sullivan operas or Sousa marches, carry it with him to bed, the bath, the car, or the Cabinet Room, all places where he tended to work, and mumble it again to himself over the course of several days. He let it stew while using it with colleagues until, finally, it would be used in public. When composing a speech, he mobilized his resources, throwing everyone into apparent disorder in what could only have seemed like "a cross between comic opera and the launching of a major offensive." And no matter how dire or poignant the occasion, he did not relinquish the pride of authorship. Following his famous blood, toil, tears, and sweat speech in May 1940, for example, he quipped to a secretary, "That got the sods."

Colville has given another vivid picture of the Churchill method: "To watch him compose some telegram or minute for dictation is to make one feel that one is present at the birth of a child, so tense is his expression, so restless his turnings from side to side, so curious the noises he emits under his breath. Then comes out some masterly sentence and finally with a 'Gimme' he takes the sheet of typewritten paper and initials it or alters it with his fountain-pen, which he holds most awkwardly halfway up the holder." The king noted: "I have studied the way in which his brain works. He tells me, more than people imagine, of his future plans & ideas & only airs them when the time is ripe."

The king's experience was no less arduous but certainly a good deal more painful. "The damned things aren't working" was his apropos remark about loudspeakers, which suddenly began working very well indeed right before he said this during the speech at Wembley that went so badly for him in 1925. His efforts to overcome his stammer are now widely known. He acquired it as a child, and it grew progressively worse. Only through hard, disciplined work with the Australian speech therapist Lionel Logue, and the constant encouragement of the queen, was he able to make progress. That his cure coincided with the onset of war and the demands on him for a public show of strength, especially by radio broadcast, must also have had something to do with it.

The king's disposition became calmer in a crisis, however excitable he was beneath, and occasionally on, the surface. The self-discipline obviously came from his peculiar upbringing as well as his naval education, where he acquired the ability not only to master fear and strain but also to demonstrate self-discipline in a social setting. For him as well as Churchill, much of that ability emerged through the deliberate use of language. "If words counted," the latter said, "we should win this war."

To say that a personality is more complex than generalizations allow is a biographical commonplace. To say that disposition conditions rather than causes action is less obvious but no less important. Together these truisms remind us that nuances of personality are sometimes indistinguishable from the means by which they develop. Robert Rhodes James has quoted Lord Randolph Churchill's shorthand depiction of Disraeli's career as similar to that of Winston's: "Failure, failure, failure, partial success, renewed failure, ultimate and complete triumph." Yet Rhodes James's conclusion has taken the man's image at face value. This was a source of his many failures, Rhodes James and others have asserted, until events dictated that it became the basis of great success. From the perspective of personality, the verdict could just as easily have been delivered the other way around. "It was Churchill's greatest deficiency in the 1930s that he was unchanged; it was to be his greatest strength in the ordeal that began on 3 September 1939." To Churchill, however, some forms of constancy—even in abstract or romantic guise—were a source of strength and merit regardless of circumstance. They allowed a reputation to work for itself. "You will have to forget a great many things," Churchill once advised Colville. "Be wise rather than well-informed. Give your opinion but not the reasons for it. Then you will have a valuable contribution to make."

Each man followed the practice of careful arrangement in the name of perfection. They sought these absolutes. Several people have noted the king's "eagle eye," for example. This was known as a Windsor family trait; his father had it as well, often commenting upon the slightest sartorial slippage as if it were a capital offense. The practice, whether intentional or not, had the effect of cowing others and making the king appear cold and critical. It offset his otherwise consistent efforts to foster a sense of camaraderie. One day, for instance, the king noticed that Air Chief Marshal Arthur Tedder "was not wearing the Africa Star. Tedder replied that he did not know if he was entitled to it, but he was not interested unless all his chaps received it. Went on to say that the decision had been taken."

"'Yes,' said the King rather testily: 'one more dammed [sic] 2 a.m. decision taken by Winston and a very silly one too.'" Here again he took after his father. George V's biographer Kenneth Rose has written:

> Perhaps he did attach too much importance to what he wore; but then he grew up in an age that cared for such things. Endowed with neither inches nor a commanding presence, [George V] made the most of his modest attributes. His hair was always brushed with care, his beard neatly trimmed and anointed with lavender water, his manicured hands protected by gloves when shooting. Almost at death's door in 1928, he insisted on sending for a looking glass. He liked to have his family round him as he completed the ritual of dressing for dinner: the winding of the watch, the touch of scent on the handkerchief, the last adjustment to white tie and Garter Star. It was as if the centuries had rolled away and the Sun King reigned once more at Versailles.

George V went to great lengths to dictate matters related to uniforms and comportment, such as ordering his grown son to take his hat off before kissing his mother at the railroad station. His son would retain the habit, at one point insisting, in the case of plans that were being drawn up for the postwar army, that he see and approve all matters pertaining to military dress.

Churchill's eye was also keen, but it tended to notice things behind the scenes or between the lines, as it were, rather than oversights per se. His attention to detail expressed itself more obliquely. He was known, for example, to pass judgment after asking just a single question. John Peck, an assistant, has recalled going to work for him.

It was the first time I had seen Winston Churchill at close range. He was sitting up in bed with a large cigar in his mouth, studying some maps. He took no notice of me, but at intervals he reached forward to stroke a fine black cat sleeping at the foot of the bed.

"Poor Pussy," he said, "poor Pussy." I stood in silence for what seemed an age, while he comforted the cat. He then said "Poor Pussy. He's just had a painful operation. His name is Nelson. So you've come to work for me."

"Yes please, Sir."

"Good, what have you got there?"

I told him. He looked through the papers. A gentle, almost paternal smile.

"Thank you very much." I was in.

The king was slower with his judgment but also struggled with a bad temper and a terrible propensity to worry, forcing calmness upon himself—often with cigarettes. Churchill's own sleeping, smoking, drinking, and eating habits—often seen to be excessive—were, with the partial exception of the final one, also like what today is popularly called self-medication.

Even in repose, Churchill's pregnant mind and restless constitution remained active. So odd were his working and meal hours, which he called "stomach" or "tummy" time, that he kept going by a fondness, acquired in Cuba during the Spanish-American War, for taking afternoon naps—absent which he could be in the foulest of moods—usually followed by a second daily bath.

Knowing this fact about his physiology helps to explain other well-known habits. Churchill has been celebrated as a great champion of the glass, and this was true, but it should be said that he rarely abused alcohol; he was a "sipper not a guzzler." He preferred champagne, brandy, and whiskey, and drank little else; and though he took it at all hours, his whiskey almost always came heavily diluted with water. Only on rare occasions did he vary, for example, during the First World War when he drank hock and received a rebuke. His riposte: "I am interning it."

A similar tendency governed his enthusiasm for tobacco. Accounts vary but most say that he rarely actually smoked; he simply kept the cigars in his mouth, or in his hand after having lit them. He certainly was neither a drunkard—as Hitler had once called him—nor a chain smoker. What he abused, if this is the correct word, was an appetite for food. He generally liked a simple English diet—especially roast beef—at any time of the day, but very little bread, as, he said, "it is nothing more than a vehicle to convey the filling to the stomach." He was not averse to more elaborate cuisines but was usually disinclined to impose limits on his diet.

More than drink, cigars, or roast beef, his greatest tonic was the rhythm of life itself, in spite of the above-mentioned belief in constancy. Change, he said, is "[a]ll that the human structure requires." He loved to change plans and change them again, which drove his military commanders mad. Rest, especially sleep, were necessities to master, not to obey. While Churchill rarely heeded anyone's advice to take a rest, he would also suggest that he had no choice in the matter, as if he were in a race to achieve as much as possible in the limited time provided to him, albeit on his own schedule, which also included long hours working in bed, generally in his favorite silk Chinese dragon dressing gown alongside his favorite cat (Nelson or "Cat, darling").

Like the king, Churchill had few permanent enemies or hatreds, although this was not true in reverse, as many people were said to hate him at given moments. He once said that "he hated nobody and didn't feel he had any enemies—except the Huns, and that was professional!" This did not mean that he was never angry. Colville observed that his temper "was like lightning and sometimes terrifying to see, but it lasted for a short time."

He could be violently offensive to those who worked for him and although he would never say he was sorry, he would equally never let the sun go down without in some way making amends or showing that he had not meant to be unkind. His sarcasm could be biting, but it was often accompanied by an engaging smile which seemed to say that no harm was really intended.

He had to be careful. The "dignity of a Prime Minister," he said, "like a lady's virtue, is not susceptible of partial diminution." Again, like the king, he spoke with the voice of the nation, or as he once put it, in reaction to Ismay's having given him credit for inspiring the British people: "Not at all. It was given to me to express what was in the[ir] hearts. . . . If I had said anything else, they would have hurled me from office." Churchill repeated the idea several times, as those who recall his line—"It was the nation and the race living all around the globe that had the lion's heart. I had the luck to be called on to give the roar"—will know.

He liked credit but only certain kinds: medals he craved; titles he abjured. He repeatedly turned down the Order of the Garter until finally persuaded to accept it in 1953, which allowed him to say "with his schoolboy's grin, 'Now Clemmie will have to be a lady at last.'" Otherwise, "I don't see why I should not have the Garter and continue to be known as Mr. Churchill," he wondered. "After all, my father was known as Lord Randolph Churchill, but he was not a Lord. That was only a courtesy title. Why should I not continue to be called Mr. Churchill as a discourtesy title?"

He nevertheless did accept the Order of Merit and the title of Lord Warden of the Cinque Ports in 1941, which allowed him to stay at Walmer Castle, Wellington's final residence, although living so close to the Channel had by then become too dangerous.

There were these occasional attempts to appear humble. They were also exaggerated, perhaps. The point is that both Churchill and the king depicted their public role as being indistinguishable from their service as symbols of the people and the nation. Both understood the value of perceptions and impressions and the significance these had on public opinion, their first audience.

Both men therefore shared the tendency to draw connections between moods, habits, dispositions, tendencies, and personality, with varying degrees of self-awareness. This was connected to their need for companionship. Churchill, especially, found it hard to be alone for too long. Ultimately, both shared the tension between the internally and the externally driven parts of their character, possibly, in extremes—because who they were (and who they knew they were) and what was, and was seen to be, expected of them came to exist in relation and in reference to each other. When they felt alone, they both had a "tendency to morbidness and introspection and self-pity." The king's only began to dissolve following his marriage. Churchill's never really did.

The king's favorite principles were the simplest: they were

consistent, he said, with his lifelong service as a freemason: "hierarchic discipline . . . dignity and simplicity of [the] ceremonial . . . [and] the simplicity and vitality of [the] three great tenets—brotherly love, relief and truth." These were the sources of his concentration, regulation, and moderation. Relaxation and stimulation for their own sake were another matter. The king's enjoyment of motoring, for example—being a "demon driver"—probably served no other purpose. Churchill's pleasures were had in five-pack bezique, the Corinthian bagatelle, and the occasional film, as well as singing. He also had a special fondness for water—of any kind. He loved to partake in exuberant baths: to "fling himself under the water, and then surface again, blowing like a whale. When he emerged from the bath Sawyers would be standing with an enormous towel, and, draped in this, the prime minister would pace to and fro, followed by [a secretary] with notebook and pencil." Unlike the king, he adored the sea. There are frequent references to his porpoise-like qualities, his bathing "like a hippopotamus in a swamp." Rarely was he bothered by any aquatic subject. Sawyers once observed him resting on top of his hot water bottle.

"That isn't at all a good idea."

"Idea? It isn't an idea, it's a coincidence."

Churchill's most celebrated hobby, finally, was painting. It may have been the only activity about which he was consistently modest: "I do not presume to explain how to paint, but only how to get enjoyment." The challenge was to avoid the tendency to "turn the superior eye of critical passivity upon" it. He continued:

> We must not be too ambitious. We cannot aspire to
> masterpieces. We may content ourselves with a joy ride in a

paint-box.... Splash into the turpentine, wallop into the blue and the white, frantic flourish on the palette—clean no longer—and then several large, fierce strokes and slashes of blue on the absolutely cowering canvas. Anyone could see that it could not hit back. No evil fate avenged the jaunty violence. The canvas grinned in helplessness before me. The spell was broken . . . I seized the largest brush and fell upon my victim with Berzerk fury. I have never felt any awe of a canvas since.

It was with painting and in tending the house, walls, and fields at Chartwell that Churchill appeared most at peace. For all that he thrived upon action, he was not immune to the need for rest and relaxation, although here, too, he was as obsessive over minute matters as in any other field—for example, taking considerable time to lay bricks or to inspect the butterflies, golden orfe, and other fauna and flora in Chartwell's gardens, small waterfalls, pools and streams, many of which he designed, dug, or built himself.

"Nobody is more lovable than he when he is in this frame of mind," Colville said, "communicative and benign." How else may one regard a wartime prime minister "snuggled down beneath the bedclothes," given his copy of Boswell's *Journal of a Tour to the Hebrides*, and then "smiling sweetly" before saying good night?

CHAPTER EIGHT

Horror

I n the fall of 1939, after the declaration of war, Churchill rejoined the government as First Lord of the Admiralty. His "fortunes ... underwent the most dramatic reversal of any politician of modern times." Chamberlain "showed me his War Cabinet," the king recorded in his diary. "Winston Churchill as 1st Lord was a surprise though I knew he would be in the War Cabinet." The next day they met. Churchill was "[v]ery pleased to be back in harness again. Wanted more destroyers."

Churchill had returned. At the Admiralty he sat at the same desk as the one he had used from 1911 until 1915. "He rushed up the steps and flung open the panelling. There were the charts. The ships were still there." In the House of Commons, he sat listening to Chamberlain and was incensed at the situation in which the country now found itself. "Once again defence of the rights of a weak State, outraged and invaded by unprovoked aggression, forced us to draw the sword. Once again we must fight for life and honour against all the might and fury of the valiant, disciplined and ruthless German race. Once again! So be it."

When, after the war, Churchill began his six-volume history of it where his earlier history *The World Crisis* had left off, he noted that the two wars were essentially one thirty-year-long conflict. So there he was, following the same practices: twice-daily reports of ship movements, weather reports—he would affix a small card-board dolphin to indicate a gale on the map—even inquiring as to size and substance of ship cargoes, the lists of recent arrestees kept by the Home Office, the rationale for personnel decisions, and any number of other statistics, at whatever hour he pleased.

Nearly everyone and everything was in its place; "normal" life had resumed. "Winston is back" was the signal flashed to the fleet. The signal "could be read both ways: the navy's memories of him were mixed, and he knew it." No matter. He set about doing what he knew best: dictating correspondence and memoranda that began "Pray inform me"; filling and emptying boxes with memoranda marked "Action this day"; exhorting bureaucrats and politicians to give him the resources he demanded; immersing himself in the details of the navy and making his presence felt with officers; planning and planning again for every conceivable contingency; touring ships and bases, meeting sailors; and arguing with his fellow members of the War Cabinet, "rather an old team," as he put it.

Whatever the continuities or resemblances, however, *this* war became something altogether different. Britain and much of the world had never seen anything so ruinous. Never before, even during the blackest hours on the western front in the last war, had anyone felt so intimately the prospect of total destruction. Never before in modern memory were so many of Europe's large cities bombed and burned to the ground; never had such power amassed on a global scale against the empire and all the assumptions of so many generations. But this all lay ahead.

In April, Churchill took over as chairman of the Military Co-ordination Committee, an unwieldy position with Chamberlain still prime minister, not only because it divided authority at the top but also because it blended oversight with operations in an ambiguous and increasingly rancorous fashion. It was otherwise known as the "Winston problem." Churchill was effectively "Deputy Prime Minister" for defense but without all the levers of power at his disposal, an arrangement that seemed designed merely to appease him and his supporters. At the same time, it suited Churchill: although he was nominally under Chamberlain, he could keep clean, or at least sufficiently undamaged, for he must have felt that he was all the country had left.

This need to avoid divisions of authority was behind Churchill's determination when he became prime minister in May 1940 to concentrate all important authority in himself by serving also as head of the Ministry of Defence and as chairman of the Conservative Party. It was significant that this was done with the king's formal support. Churchill now sought to control all the levers of national power, military as well as political, so as to ensure against, he would have said, the heavy liability of the last war. Yet he was not, nor could he ever be, the head of state.

However great his reputation, however deep his commitment to winning the war, or however complete his mastery of its details had become, Churchill was always a formal step beneath Roosevelt and Stalin, the leaders of his nation's two allies. (There was also an official head of state in the Soviet Union, Mikhail Kalinin, but he was really a nominal figure, in every sense.) Britain had been in the weakest, or at least the most vulnerable, position of the three. However much Churchill was regarded as their equal or even—in many instances, by age and experience—their superior, he would always be a minister. Etiquette, especially toasts at the conferences of the Big Three, had to take this fact into account. It was occasionally curious, and at other times awkward, that the heads of two nominally revolutionary states were obliged to toast an absent British king.

Did this really matter? It did and it did not. Should it have mattered? Perhaps. Few people questioned Churchill's preeminence, least of all the two allies. Yet in the back of their mind there was the existence of another authority that could challenge a particular decision. Nearer the front of Churchill's mind must have been the same notion. Of the many reasons weighing in favor of his close alliance with the king, surely the king's public support was one of the most important. That there is so little evidence of anyone attempting to overstep Churchill with his monarch is as much, or perhaps even more, a result of the king's own trust in his position with the prime minister as it is of the latter's diligence in satisfying the king's need for inclusion. Yet even Roosevelt, shortly before his death, was overheard muttering to himself while "staring into space, and apparently completely absorbed in his own thoughts. He only spoke three times (not to the visitor but as if to himself)—'If Churchill insists on Hongkong, I will have to take it to the King.' This was repeated three times."

"I must warn you that you are approaching a head-on smash in Norway," Churchill began a letter to Chamberlain on April 24, 1940, then deleted the line. Did he foresee the events of the next month? He had been a loyal if argumentative member of Chamberlain's cabinet. Following the failed attempt to expel the Germans from Narvik, which, in an echo of the Dardanelles, foundered on a maldistribution of resources, Churchill could claim that his plans had been thwarted by colleagues and underlings. ("You admirals [are] all the same . . . agree on plans . . . when it comes to fighting you're yellow"—which was not true in this case.) But he withheld public criticism. "It was the only time in my life," he said, "when I have kept my mouth shut."

Some worried whether Narvik and the failure of related operations would tarnish him or perhaps, at some level, if he was still up to the job and if it had been a mistake to recall him. The more immediate problem had to do with Chamberlain. The Norwegian disaster proved fatal to what was left of his career. Back in the House of Commons, Chamberlain "sat there, his dark figure erect," observed a witness, Edward Spears:

> Then he stood up. He held himself very straight. The whole House watched him as he looked for a moment at the Assembly that had dealt him such a grievous blow, the last and most significant thrust of the many cruel ones delivered during two days of almost unrelieved attack. He often gave the misleading impression that he was sneering owing to the way his nostrils lifted when he smiled or even spoke. Such an expression flitted on his face for a moment, then froze into a more usual one of cold aloofness, almost of distaste. . . . He walked out of the House and through the lobby with heavy feet, a truly sad and pathetic figure.

Churchill would escape punishment; indeed, he would prevail in the moment. History did not repeat itself, not this time. He would remain wedded to—some would say fixated on—"mad plans" for a Norwegian front for some time to come, but this was not to happen the way he wanted, in good part because the chiefs, Brooke especially, did not get the point of his interest in it. Now, at last, though, he became prime minister. Other fronts, namely France, became paramount.

France was on the eve of defeat. On an earlier occasion—his capture by a Boer patrol—Churchill had recalled the words of Napoleon: "When one is alone and unarmed, a surrender may be pardoned." Not this time. Britain stood alone but she was not a prisoner. She was not defeated. Nor would she be destroyed. But Hitler's armies had begun their conquest. The Sitzkrieg, or Phony War, was over. The real war that so many had feared had begun. "There were many people in this country who looked on quite happily while Herr Hitler stripped leaf after leaf from the European artichoke," Harold Nicolson has written, "and who contended that it was not merely fit and proper that he should obtain this satisfaction but that he would be so charmed, so 'satiated,' by the outer leaves that he would discard the choke and not proceed to examine the succulent receptacle which would remain behind." Not so. "There are very few leaves left upon that artichoke today." Churchill, however, was in a fine mood. Spears saw him

sitting relaxed and rotund in an arm-chair at his desk. He offered me a cigar, looked at me for a moment as if I were a lens through which he was gazing at something beyond, then the kindliest, friendliest expression spread over his face as he focused on me, his face puckered into a lovable baby-like grin, then he was grave again.

Churchill's first efforts were to stiffen the morale of the French and to see for himself the conditions of the French army. He was known to be a fond Francophile who saw that country as being synonymous with civilization. He took several trips across the Channel, each one seeming more obviously dire than the previous, to do what he could to avert the country's collapse. Ismay recalled the final scene in June 1940:

A bare room in a disused chateau on the Loire. The actors— the French and British High Commands, seated round a long table. General Weygand describing the desperate plight of the French Army, and pleading that all fighter aircraft in England should be sent to their aid.

"Here," said the General, "is the decisive point, now is the decisive moment. Nothing must be held back. Everything must be hurled into battle."

A terrible moment for Winston Churchill, a great lover of France and the most loyal and generous of friends. A long pause, and then the measured reply: "No. This is not the decisive point or the decisive moment. That will come when Hitler hurls his bombers against Great Britain. If we can keep command of the air over our islands, and if we can keep the seas open, as we certainly shall do, we will win it all back for you."

And then a characteristic gesture of chivalry and defiance— "But if you think it best for France in her agony that her Army should capitulate, let there be no hesitation on our account.

Whatever happens here, we shall fight on for ever and ever and ever. I pledge you my word that Britain will never surrender."

M. Reynaud, obviously touched, said: "But if our Army surrenders, the whole might of Germany will be turned upon you and they will invade you. Then what will you do?"

Back whipped the reply: "I haven't thought that out very carefully, but, broadly speaking I should propose to drown as many as possible of them on the way over, and then to knock on the head any that managed to crawl ashore."

The French generals Maurice Gamelin and Maxime Weygand had begged him for men, money, supplies, and aircraft—especially aircraft. How things had changed from the moment in 1936 when Weygand had said he would want six divisions from England if France were again at war with Germany. Weygand characterized the situation now simply as "a race between the exhaustion of the French and the shortness of breath of the enemy divisions." Churchill "hunched over the table, his face flushed, was watching Weygand intently. His expression," Spears observed, "was not benevolent." He tried using the French language, his own particular fluent if idiosyncratic form of "frog speech." Weygand seemed by now to want to capitulate, and Marshal Pétain looked hopeless. Gamelin just shrugged.

Churchill had ordered the British Expeditionary Force (BEF) sent to keep the French viable. It arrived at the end of 1939 and was unable to do much of anything for French military strength, especially because the British had withheld—by necessity—sending most of the air force as well. At this point the BEF could only prepare for its own retreat. Unfortunately, as Dill telephoned to Brooke, "The Prime Minister does not want you to do that." Brooke replied, "What the hell does he want?" Churchill then picked up the receiver and told Brooke that he "had been sent to France to make the French feel that we were supporting them." Brooke "replied that it was impossible to make a corpse feel." The conversation went back and forth, until, "at last," when Brooke "was in an exhausted condition," Churchill finally said, "All right. I agree with you!" The general could be forgiven for concluding that "it is the only time in all the work we subsequently did together that he made use of those words."

"Nothing but a miracle can save the BEF now," Brooke had written in May, as it proceeded to Dunkirk. Churchill said, "Of course, whatever happens at Dunkirk we shall fight on"; the enemy, in another of his favorite phrases, must "bleed and burn." The king took to recording the number of evacuees in his diary over the course of the operation. He was not incapable of seeing a silver lining. He wrote to his mother, "Personally I feel happier now that we have no allies to be polite to & to pamper." Then he added in his diary, "I always feel that we have to be thankful France collapsed at once after Dunkirk, so that we were able to reorganize the Army at home, & gave us time to prepare the Air Force to repel the Blitzkrieg."

The French fleet continued to preoccupy Churchill. When it was suggested that the French might keep it or, even worse, let it fall to the Germans, he was adamant: "Tell them that if they let us have their fleet we shall never forget, but that if they surrender without consulting us we shall never forgive. We shall blacken their name for a thousand years!" He later retracted that statement but still said to Admiral Jean-François Darlan, the French commander, "Darlan, you must never let them get the French Fleet." This sentiment was endorsed from an unexpected source:

Dear Prime Minister

Why not declare war on France and capture her fleet (which would gladly strike its colors to us) before A.H. recovers his breath?

Surely that is the logic of the situation?

Tactically,
G. Bernard Shaw.

The British went on to destroy the fleet. Darlan was later assassinated under mysterious circumstances.

By June, France had fallen. There was now "a rift between us, a slight crack in the crystal cup sufficient to change its sound when touched," recalled Spears. "I had my password and they did not have theirs. We no longer belonged to one society bounded by the same horizon. A lifetime steeped in French feeling, sentiment and affection was falling from me. England alone counted now."

The fall of France meant a whole new kind of war from the one fought there previously. On the whole, there were only three ways to win it: blockade, bombing, and insurgency. There seemed to be little in any of these efforts that France could offer, with the partial exception of the third, but the French should not be abused for all that they had lost. Churchill had to remind colleagues that "[s]o far the French had had nine-tenths of the casualties . . . and endured ninety-nine-hundredths of the suffering." Magnanimity in defeat, alas—even in the defeat of one's own ally. To the king he wrote, "Better days will come—though not yet."

The king had been keeping busy from the outset of the war in the way that his father had prepared him: reading papers, talking with ministers, visiting factories, hospitals, and troops. He often seemed to want to be doing more. That he had felt the same way during the previous war no doubt did not help: "Everyone," he wrote, was "working at fever heat except me."

He did what he could closest to home. He carried a rifle and a revolver, and both he and the queen took up shooting practice in Buckingham Palace Gardens, possibly forgetting that they had allowed their friend Halifax and his wife to walk there whenever they liked without warning. He also tried to establish rapport with Churchill, but not so easily at first. Halifax reported that the king was "funny about Winston, and told me he did not find him very easy to talk to. Nor was Winston willing to give him as much time, or information, as he would like." This appeared in a couple of other accounts, including the king's diary from nine months before: "Winston is difficult to talk to but in time I shall get the right technique I hope." The difficulty was compounded by Churchill's failure to be punctual, keeping both Their Majesties waiting over an hour on more than one occasion.

Thus in September the two resolved to hold their weekly lunches. The dramatic events culminating in the Dunkirk evacuation had done much to bring them together, as Churchill had kept the king well informed during the ordeal. They fell into a pattern, so much so that the king could write to his mother, "I am getting to know Winston better, & I feel that we are beginning to understand each other. . . .

Winston is definitely the right man at the helm at the moment." From the other side of the wall, on another occasion, their "two tongues" were heard "wagging like mad!"

Churchill continued: "King George and Queen Elizabeth are a far finer, more popular and more inspiringly helpful pair than the other [Edward VIII and Wallis] would have been. We could not have a better King and Queen in Britain's most perilous hour." And Colville observed, "Relations between the King and the Prime Minister soon became excellent. . . . [E]ven Queen Mary developed an immense admiration for Winston. . . . As the war proceeded the King and Queen became as devoted to Winston Churchill as he consistently was to them."

A high priority for both leaders was to secure the support of the United States. This was a frustrating task, and one to be tackled with much diplomacy. Typical was the view of the king back in 1938: "The U.S.A. must be left alone. They will never take a more active line if we preach at them." But something had to be done. The writer Eve Curie put her finger on the difficulty when she addressed the Americans: "If you have been helping these people for their sake, what you are doing is magnificent, but if you are doing it to protect yourselves it is not nearly enough!" The United States wished the British well but within limits that nobody, not even Churchill, could expect to remove immediately. On the other hand, there was a mutual interest, even logic of alliance, that both Churchill and the king were determined to exploit. In September 1939 the king had remonstrated with Ambassador Kennedy, notorious then for his isolationism:

As I see it, the U.S.A., France & the British Empire are the three really free peoples in the World, & two of these great democracies are now fighting against all that we three countries hate & detest. . . . England, my country . . . has been expected to act & has had to act. . . . The British Empire has once again shown to the World a united front in this coming struggle. . . . The British Empire's mind is made up. I leave it at that.

There was more to be done. One day, Randolph entered his father's bedroom. The prime minister

was standing in front of his basin and shaving with his old fashioned Valet razor. . . . "Sit down, dear boy, and read the papers while I finish shaving."

I did as told. After two or three minutes of hacking away, he half turned and said: "I think I see my way through." He resumed his shaving. I was astonished, and said: "Do you mean that we can avoid defeat? (which seemed credible) or beat the bastards?" (which seemed incredible).

He flung his Valet razor into the basin, swung around and said:—

"Of course I mean we can beat them."

"Well, I'm all for it, but I don't see how you can do it."

By this time he had dried and sponged his face and turning round to me, said with great intensity: "I shall drag the United States in."

Luckily Franklin Roosevelt was less bald than Mussolini, who once used similar phraseology—"trying to drag me into the war by the hair"—regarding Hitler and his attempt to entice Italy into an alliance. So single-minded was Churchill's determination for American ships, whose value was "measured in rubies," that a cartoon once showed the king in bed with a glum expression. "George, why do you look so low this morning?" asked the queen. "Because I have it on the best authority that Winston means to swap me for an old destroyer." When it was later suggested following the U.S. intervention that there would be an accounting for all the aid the Americans had given, Churchill replied happily, "But I shall have my account to put in too and my account is for holding the baby alone for eighteen months, and it was a very rough brutal baby I had to hold. I don't quite know what I shall have to charge for it."

For now the United States was of two minds. This included the president, evidently. Roosevelt wrote to a friend and former teacher, the Harvard professor Roger Merriman:

I wish the British would stop this "We who are about to die, salute thee" attitude. Lord Lothian was here the other day, started the conversation by saying he had completely abandoned his former belief that Hitler could be dealt with as a semi-reasonable human being, and went on to say that the British for a thousand years had been the guardians of Anglo-Saxon civilization—that the scepter or the sword or something like that had dropped from their palsied fingers—that the U.S.A. must snatch it up—that F.D.R. alone could save the world—etc., etc.

I got mad clear through and told him that just so long as he or Britishers like him took that attitude of complete despair, the British would not be worth saving anyway.

What the British need today is a good stiff grog, inducing not only the desire to save civilization but the continued belief that they can do it. In such an event they will have a lot more support from their American cousins—don't you think so?

Churchill liked to say he was half American, which was nominally the case, since his mother was born in the United States. He had visited America a few times and had American cousins and friends. He had some sympathy for, but little mastery of, the country's politics, had never lived there for any extended period, and had almost no exposure to the American president, whom he had only met once many years before. He did not even recall this meeting when Roosevelt reminded him of it. Now Roosevelt was the indispensable man and Churchill was determined to woo him. He was less successful with Eleanor, who was once heard to say that Churchill was "sixty years out of date." Wooing the president may seem in retrospect to be easier than it was at the time, and without the arch-facilitator, Roosevelt's assistant Harry Hopkins—"Lord Root of the Matter," as Churchill called him—it might never have happened. Hopkins quoted Scripture to describe what he would say to the president: "'Whither thou goest, I will go; and where thou lodgest, I will lodge: thy people shall be my people, and thy God my God.'

"Then he added very quietly, 'Even to the end.'" Churchill was in tears when he heard it.

That Churchill succeeded in this effort probably had as much to do with Roosevelt's storied temperament and his belief in the Allied cause as it did with Churchill's charm, as compelling as it was. The king and the queen had also helped pave the way.

In the spring and summer of 1939 they had toured Canada and the United States. They were the first royals to visit the latter since American independence, though strictly speaking the king had already been there some years before when he briefly stepped across the border on a trip to Niagara Falls. They had been told that indeed the Americans were "the greatest worshippers of Royalty," but the two did not like the idea of leaving home at that particular moment, and may have felt overly conscious of the popularity of the Duke and Duchess of Windsor in America. The visit was nonetheless an achievement. They nipped isolationism in the bud—in Canada at least, where they were engulfed by veterans "weeping, and crying, 'Ay, man, if Hitler could just see this.' The American correspondents were simply staggered. . . . It was a wonderful example of what true democracy means, and a people's king."

Farther south they endured the terrible heat but rallied to impress not only the American people but also, most important, Roosevelt, who had dismissed the two before as merely "two nice young people." Perhaps these were his true feelings. Or perhaps he was influenced by memoranda such as the following one from his ambassador to France, William Bullitt:

> I have the honor to submit herewith to the Chief of State in accordance with his request . . . the recommendations as to the personal needs of Their Royal Majesties, George VI and Elizabeth, King and Queen, By the Grace of God, of Great

Britain, Ireland and of the British Dominions Beyond the Seas, King and Queen Defender of the Faith, Emperor and Empress of India.

I may add that my most onerous diplomatic labor since reaching Paris has been the extraction of these recommendations and that I expect you to decorate me at once with the Order of the Royal Bathtub.

At Hyde Park the president greeted them with cocktails. "My mother thinks you should have a cup of tea; she doesn't approve of cocktails." The king replied, "Neither does my mother," and took one. They spent many more hours discussing the world's perils in detail, including several proposals relating to Atlantic bases and patrols. "He is so easy to get to know," the king wrote of Roosevelt, "& never makes one feel shy." When asked if American support would be forthcoming later on, the king replied, "It's in the bag."

Not quite. It would take some more time before Churchill could say of Roosevelt, "He's my baby now!" The war could not be won without the help of the Americans, and if it were lost, Churchill later said to a visiting American congressman, "with dying hands we shall pass on the torch to you." Like his earlier outburst at Kennedy and Lippmann, the threat probably inspired little confidence.

The results of this journey were not minimal, however. To Colville, they "had made America give up its partisanship of the Windsors." For the king personally, it was an important achievement and "a roaring success." The cheering of the crowds impressed him deeply. In Canada, he acknowledged not only the mere symbol of the British Crown ... [but also] the institutions which have developed, century after century, beneath the aegis of the Crown; institutions, British in origin, British in their slow and almost casual growth, which, because they are grounded root and branch on British faith in liberty and justice, mean more to us even than the splendour of our history or the glories of our English tongue.

The king continued to do his part for Anglo-American relations once the war began. He wrote to Roosevelt on matters of concern, along with the occasional proposal—for example, for common preparation of relief and reconstruction for postwar Europe—and welcomed the new American ambassador, John "Gil" Winant, at the station when he arrived at Windsor on a special train sent for him. Winant described it as "the first time in the history of Great Britain that a King had gone to meet an Ambassador. . . . He was returning the courtesy which President Roosevelt had shown Lord Halifax and I didn't even have a battleship!" The statement alluded to the quiet role that the king played in encouraging the destroyers-for-bases deal during his visit to America. He would persist with such acts of diplomacy, sending morale-boosting messages to Eisenhower and welcoming a retinue of Americans over the course of the war. By April 1942 the king himself would travel to Downing Street to dine with Churchill, Hopkins, and General Marshall. Lest Roosevelt ever begin to lose faith, the king took to reminding him that "Mr. Churchill . . . is indefatigable at his work. . . . He is a great man, & has at last come into his own as leader of his country in this fateful time in her history. I have every confidence in him."

The Phony War had ended. "Now at last," according to Churchill, "the slowly-gathered, long-pent-up fury of the storm broke upon us." Then came the Blitz.

It was not only the industrial East End that was hit. Holland House was almost entirely destroyed. Bombs damaged the Privy Council chamber, windows in the Foreign Office, the Treasury, and 10 Downing Street, as well as Bedford House in Belgrave Square and the Carlton Club. The area around St. Paul's Cathedral, so miraculously spared, was, according to the diarist James Lees-Milne, "like wandering in Pompeii . . . like scarred flesh, and as yet untoned by time." When the chamber of the House of Commons was hit, the members were forced to meet in the House of Lords, with the latter moving to the King's Robing Room. Number 10 was no longer safe. Churchill one day poked the ceiling with his stick and it entered directly with almost no resistance. He took to sleeping in the Cabinet War Rooms, his offices near Downing Street; others slept there in the shelter below. New rooms, which were called the Annexe, were later set up above them. Brooke moved to his new office, deep underground, which was supplied with all the best technology but had one drawback, he said: "Its proximity to Winston!" Churchill was pleased with his, which he introduced to Brooke "just like a small boy showing his new toy and all it could do!"

Such playacting was common and hard, in fact, to distinguish from real acting. Brooke "was convulsed watching [Churchill] give this exhibition of bayonet exercises, dressed up in his romper suit and standing in the ancestral hall of Chequers." "I remember wondering," he wrote, "what Hitler would have made of this demonstration of skill at arms." On one of his trips to France, he demanded to his detective, "Get my heavy pistol for me. If we are attacked on the way I may be able to kill at least one German." On others closer to home, "Bang, bang, bang, goes the farmer's gun, run rabbit, run rabbit, run, run, run," Churchill chanted. "I love the bang." There is a related picture, drawn by Halifax, of "Winston in his dugout":

> He was exactly like a thing on the stage in what I understand nurses are accustomed to call "a romper suit" of Air Force colour Jaeger-like stuff, with a zipp fastening up the middle, and a little Air Force forage cap. I asked him if he was going on the stage but he said he always wore this in the morning. It is really almost like Goering.

An interest in airpower may have been one of the few things Churchill shared with Hermann Goering, but it was an important one. It dated to his time as air minister after the last war. However, if one were to view airpower as a type of cavalry, it would have gone back to the very beginning of his military service and could not be considered separately from the "triphibious" concept that involved the maximum use of all services on the land, sea, and in the air. "What is the use," he asked, "of having the command of the sea if it is not to pass troops to and fro with great rapidity from one theatre to another?" And what is the use of having command of the air? Britain may have been the "great amphibian," but this identity, like his own, was now in flux, as described in chapter six, during difficult exchanges between him and his military commanders. Brooke did not underestimate airpower but felt its role had to be coordinated with great care. The Norwegian losses, for example, were to him "the first real conclusive proof we have had of the undermining of sea power by air power." According to Portal, who ought to have known, Churchill "never really understood the air." Understanding and acceptance were two different things in this instance. He could on occasion seem coldblooded indeed about strategic bombing. He predicted that tourists "who go to Italy to look at ruins won't have to go as far as Naples and Pompeii in future." Upon learning that Athens had been bombed, he replied "without hesitation . . . 'Then we must bomb Rome [where] it wouldn't hurt the Coliseum to have a few more bricks knocked off it.'" How these feelings were or were not affected by the Blitz cannot be known for certain. It was an experience that nobody who has not been through it can truly know. In any event, for the foreseeable future, much of the war took place in the air. Colville noted a typical day, September 17, 1940:

> We lunched off beer and bottled tongue and then I went down to the House to hear the P.M. make a statement on the air-raids, etc. Just as he was about to speak, the spotters on the roof (who now supplement air-raid warnings by blowing whistles when the enemy are really near) became active and the House of Commons repaired to its dug-outs. I remained in my room having so far preserved a healthy contempt for these alarums and excursions—except after dark when the shell splinters fly. . . . 8.00 p.m. is about zero-hour for the night raid and the accompanying gun fire.

Churchill went to inspect bomb damage at Peckham, and saw little Union Jacks displayed in the rubble. He began to cry, he said, from "wonder and admiration." As extraordinary as it must have been, people became so used to the terror that it became almost second nature as their cities, especially London, which bore much of the onslaught, came to feel in some ways more alive than ever. Eventually it all seemed par for the course. Churchill once was heard to ask:

"What was that noise?"

"I think it was a bomb, Sir."

"That is a platitude."

There was a great deal of confusion. Once, for example, a "policeman tried to arrest [Churchill] for having too bright side-lights and was finally dismissed with a loud 'Go to Hell, man.'" The king appeared to seek out these encounters and was said to relish being asked for his identity card. Churchill took to watching the bombs fall from the rooftops whenever he could, once causing an influx of smoke down below while sitting on top of the chimney. When members of his staff protested his causing or daring disaster, he replied:

"My time will come when it comes."

"'You're probably right, sir,' came a dejected voice from the darkness, 'but there's no need to take half a dozen of us with you.'"

Danger enlivened him:

"Pugnacious old bugger, ain't he?"

The "unconventional tribute from the ranks" on one of his troop walkabouts "delighted" Churchill. As did the remark of a workman as he walked past on another, "There goes the bloody British Empire."

"*Very* nice," he said quietly.

"Good old Winnie. . . . We can take it. Give it 'em back." Then an old woman among them was heard to say, "You see, he really cares; he's crying."

"Poor people, poor people," he said. "They trust me and I can give them nothing but disaster for a long long time."

The king and queen also toured bombed areas, prompting "admiration" (for him) and "adoration" (for her): "Oh, ain't she lovely; ain't she just *bloody* lovely!" Their trips to the East End and other, mainly poor, neighborhoods, showed them at their sympathetic best. The images of these visits, like Churchill's, are among the most durable in the public mind. Empathy would presently join sympathy. On September 9, 1940, and then again three days later, Buckingham Palace was bombed, and in the second instance, the king and queen were in actual danger. They insisted upon remaining in London whenever they could, and now it was their turn to be hit. The king described the moment:

We went to London (from Windsor) & found an Air Raid in progress. The day was very cloudy & it was raining hard. The Queen & I went upstairs to a small sitting room overlooking the Quadrangle. (I could not use my usual sitting room owing to the broken windows by former bomb damage.) All of a sudden we heard the zooming noise of a diving aircraft getting louder & louder & then saw 2 bombs falling past the opposite side of Buck. Palace into the Quadrangle. We saw the flashes & heard the detonation as they burst about 30 yds away. The blast blew in the windows opposite to us, & 2 great craters had appeared in the Quadrangle. From one of these craters water from a burst main was pouring out & flowing into the passage through the broken windows. The whole thing happened in a matter of seconds & we were very quickly out into the passage.

There were 6 bombs. 2 in the Forecourt, 2 in the Quadrangle. 1 wrecked the Chapel & 1 in the garden.

The queen had just begun to remove "an eyelash out of the eye" of the king when they

> heard the unmistakable whirr-whirr of a German plane. We said, "ah a German," and before anything else could be said, there was the noise of aircraft diving at great speed, and then the scream of a bomb. It all happened so quickly, that we had only time to look foolishly at each other, when the scream hurtled past us, and exploded with a tremendous crash in the quadrangle. . . . I saw a great column of smoke & earth thrown up into the air, and then we all ducked like lightning into the corridor. There was another tremendous explosion, and we & our 2 pages who were outside the door, remained for a moment or two in the corridor away from the staircase, in case of flying glass. It is curious how one's instinct works at these moments of great danger. . . . Everybody remained wonderfully calm, and we went down to the shelter. I went along to see if the housemaids were alright.

All in all, the palace was hit nine times.

The Blitz continued, with the queen making her famous "we can look the East End in the face" comment and the king celebrating their "new bond" with the people, but there was little doubt that they, and especially he, were affected deeply by the attacks on the palace. "It was a ghastly experience & I don't want it to be repeated."

He later established a new honor—the George Cross and Medal, given to civilians for bravery during air raids.

It would get worse. There were nearly a thousand casualties in Coventry, which was almost entirely destroyed. The king made it a priority to go there as soon as he could to see the damage. He would continue on to Southampton, Birmingham, and Bristol, demonstrating as best he could his solidarity with the victims, undertaking, according to one account, some fifty thousand miles of travel within Britain alone. The king also continued with his weekly investitures, and insisted on flying the royal standard to show his presence.

The royal family had their air-raid shelter in the palace, which appeared to be an "immense catacomb" decorated haphazardly with "gilt chairs, a regency settee . . . a large Victorian mahogany table . . . [and] many of the valuable small Dutch landscapes which had been brought downstairs." The king continued to sleep at the palace and rejected proposals to evacuate the family, including his daughters, saying he would be happy to lead a resistance movement against any invading Germans. Nicolson recalled a related conversation with the queen on the subject of patriotism:

> "That is what keeps us going. I should die if I had to leave." She also told me that she is being instructed every morning how to fire a revolver. I expressed surprise. "Yes," she said, "I shall not go down like the others." I cannot tell you how superb she was. But I anticipated her charm. What astonished me is how the King has changed. I always thought him rather a foolish loutish boy. He is now like his brother. . . . He was so gay and

she was so calm...those two resolute and sensible. WE SHALL WIN. I know that. I have no doubts at all.

The staff made extensive plans. The exiled King Haakon of Norway once asked to see them in action. What if German paratroopers landed and tried to kidnap the king? The king said he would sound the alarm and see. He did and nothing happened. Since the police were not aware of any attack, they dismissed the alarm, but when told what had been done, they sent several men to hunt for intruders in the shrubbery.

The palace itself was grim. When Eleanor Roosevelt visited it in the fall of 1942, she was struck by its wartime appearance and austere condition, with wooden coverings on the missing windows— even in the queen's bedroom, where she stayed—and the lack of heat and hot water, as well as the poor quality of the food (fish cakes, cold ham and chicken, and Brussels sprouts) served on gold and silver plates. The bathtubs had marks at the five-inch level, and reminders to conserve water and electricity were posted in all the bathrooms. Both the king and the queen, she observed, suffered from bad colds.

The resolution of the king and queen grew in direct proportion to their bleak surroundings. Halifax recalled a luncheon

à trois, quite easy and informal. They both struck me in good form. My admiration for them grows daily. After luncheon when I was talking to the King, he looked at the clock and said "By summer time 1.52. The time to the minute at which I took over four years ago."

This was back in December 1940. Britain had endured the worst six months in anyone's memory. On a tour of the Swansea docks some weeks later, Churchill appeared before the shell-shocked crowd, which soon converged on him, alarming his guards. "Stand back my men—let the others have a chance to see too." Then he stuck his bowler hat onto the edge of his cane, and thrust it into the air.

"Let no one be mistaken," the king had said the previous May, "it is no mere territorial conquest that our enemies are seeking. It is the overthrow, complete and final, of this Empire and of everything for which it stands, and after that the conquest of the world. . . . Against our honesty is set dishonour, against our faithfulness is set treachery, against our justice, brute force. There, in clear and unmistakable opposition, lie the forces which now confront one another." They had made it to the end of the most trying year. "We had not flinched or wavered," Churchill later wrote. "We had not failed. . . . All our latent strength was now alive. . . . The Battle of Britain was won. The Battle of the Atlantic had now to be fought."

CHAPTER NINE

Reversal

It is said that war is a succession of periods of boredom interspersed by the occasional moment of terror. As between "slow-time" and "tank-time" there are few gradations in combat. This may be the experience for many among the rank and file. Not for Churchill. He welcomed constant action.

War almost never happens that way. Rather, there is a cycle of gains, losses, and frustration, right up to the very end and even through the aftermath. War may later appear, as it does in Churchill's histories, as the unveiling of a heroic plot, reaching a climax. In the moment, however, there was adversity of a different order: less a contest of strength than, increasingly, one of endurance, reminding us of Rudyard Kipling's advice about dealing with triumph and disaster: "And treat those two impostors just the same."

There were three general phases of this war: the period from fall 1939 to spring 1940, or the Phony War; the year from June 1940 to June 1941 when Britain fought for its survival, more or less alone; and the subsequent phase beginning with the German attack on the Soviet Union and lasting to the end in 1945.

Near the middle of the second phase, Churchill and the king were amazed, emboldened, yet deeply chastened, by their ordeal. The king, staying at Sandringham, sent his prime minister his

best wishes for a happier New Year, & may we see the end of this conflict in sight during the coming year [1941]. I am already feeling better for my sojourn here, it is doing me good, & the change of scene & outdoor exercise is acting as a good tonic. But I feel that it is wrong for me to be away from my place of duty, when everybody else is carrying on. However I must look upon it as medicine & hope to come back refreshed in mind & body, for renewed efforts against the enemy.

I do hope & trust you were able to have a little relaxation at Xmas with all your arduous work. I have so much admired all you have done during the last seven months as my Prime Minister, & I have so enjoyed our talks together during our weekly luncheons. I hope they will continue on my return as I do look forward to them so much. . . .

It was indeed kind of you to help me with my broadcast on Xmas day, & very many thanks for the Siren Suit.

Churchill replied with a warm yet formal tone that had by now become typical:

I am honoured by Your Majesty's most gracious letter. The kindness with which Your Majesty and the Queen have treated me since I became First Lord and still more since I became Prime Minister has been a continuous source of strength and encouragement during the vicissitudes of this fierce struggle for life. I have already served Your Majesty's father and grandfather for a good many years as a Minister of the Crown, and my father and grandfather served Queen Victoria, but Your Majesty's treatment of me has been intimate and generous to a degree that I had never deemed possible.

Indeed, sir, we have passed through days and weeks as trying and as momentous as any in the history of the English Monarchy, and even now there stretches before us a long, forbidding road. I have been greatly charmed by our weekly luncheons in poor old bombed-battered Buckingham Palace, and to feel that in Your Majesty and the Queen there flames the spirit that will never be daunted by peril, nor wearied by unrelenting toil. This has drawn the Throne and the people more closely together than was ever before recorded, and Your Majesties are more beloved by all classes and conditions than any of the princes of the past. I am indeed proud that it should have fallen to my lot and duty to stand at Your Majesty's side as First Minister in such a climax of the British story.

———

The spring of 1941 came hard. Churchill was more depressed than usual. The only bright side was his conviction that the course of the war would soon be decided. But the mood shifted by midsummer. One of his favorite phrases—"Keep buggering on"—now prompted a new retort:

"Ah yes, Mr. Prime Minister, but you can't go on fighting rearguard actions all the time!"

Yes, there was hope. Russia was still in the war, barely, but had begun to show signs of a capacity to persevere for another couple of months, while Roosevelt's envoy Harry Hopkins had told him in March that the United States would soon enter the war.

Clemmie had been unsure. "Jock, do you think we are going to win?" she asked Colville.

"Yes."

So did Brooke. He recalled that in June he thought that "Russia would not last long, possibly 3 or 4 months, possibly slightly longer" but England was still "safe from invasion during 1941." Some optimism was still in order.

In August, Churchill traveled to Newfoundland on HMS *Prince of Wales* for his first wartime meeting with Roosevelt. On the journey he read books by C. S. Forester and watched the film *Lady Hamilton*. In Placentia Bay the two ships approached each other amid the melodies of "The Star-Spangled Banner" and "God Save the King." Churchill, in blue naval uniform, saluted, then boarded USS *Augusta* and approached Roosevelt, with beaming smile, hat, and summer suit, his body being held up by his son Elliott.

"At long last, Mr. President."

"Glad to see you aboard, Mr. Churchill."

The two shook hands and then Churchill gave FDR a letter from the king, which read, in part:

This is just a line to bring you my best wishes, and to say how glad I am that you have an opportunity at last of getting to know my Prime Minister. I am sure you will agree that he is a very remarkable man, and I have no doubt that your meeting will prove to be of great benefit to our two countries in the pursuit of our common goal.

The two went belowdecks and got down to business. "I need not tell you," Roosevelt later wrote to the king, "that we make a perfectly matched team in harness and out—and incidentally we had lots of fun together as we always do." They dined on smoked salmon, caviar, turtle soup, roast grouse, "coupe Jean d'arc" [*sic*], broiled spring chicken, buttered sweet peas, spinach omelet, candied sweet potatoes, chocolate ice cream, cookies, and cupcakes. Churchill toasted Roosevelt and Roosevelt toasted the king. They sang hymns chosen by Churchill—"For Those in Peril on the Sea," "Onward, Christian Soldiers," and "O God, Our Help in Ages Past."

Churchill delivered a detailed briefing on his return to the king, who sounded impressed with the "very blun[t]" talks. The prime minister also delivered a letter from Roosevelt, written during the conference and extending his regrets that the king, too, was not there to participate. The king must have been relieved, less because he had not taken part or in some way stood watch over the encounter but more because he was aware, like Churchill, of the tremendous necessity of American aid: "Now that Winston has returned, I am going away to Balmoral for a real change. . . . I need it in every way."

So did Churchill, evidently. Just a few weeks later he bemoaned the state of affairs: "'The Army won't fight. . . . The Army always wants more divisions, more equipment.' Said that he had 'sacked Wavell,' and now he would 'sack Dill and go himself.' Dill was of no use, little better than Wavell, etc. etc."

Wavell griped in turn, "Winston is always expecting rabbits to come out of empty hats . . . an unreasonable genius is this Winston."

Back in Washington, Halifax had reported in November that the American secretary of state, Cordell Hull, "evidently thinks that he may find himself at war with Japan at any time without much notice. I still remain completely sceptical ... but I am quite prepared to be proved wrong at any moment." Nearly two weeks later, Churchill was at Chequers with Winant and Harriman. Harriman recalled that "during dinner, at nine o'clock Sawyers ... would always bring in a small radio, a present from Harry Hopkins. It turned on by lifting the lid." Churchill, he remembered, "was a bit despondent that evening and was immersed in his thoughts." On the radio "the news started with unimportant events ... a number of items about the fighting on the Russian front and on the British front in Libya. . . ."

"Suddenly there was a pause and the announcer said he had a special dispatch. 'The Japanese have bombed Pearl Harbour.'" Churchill remembered that he "did not personally sustain any direct impression, but Averell said there was something about the Japanese attacking the Americans, and, in spite of being tired and resting, we all sat up."

"What's this about bombing Pearl Harbour?" Harriman asked.

"Tommy [Thompson, Churchill's aide] said, no, it was Pearl River." Harriman disagreed. Then Sawyers, "who had heard what had passed, came into the room, saying, 'It's quite true. We heard it ourselves outside. The Japanese have attacked the Americans.'"

Churchill jumped into action after a brief silence. So they would go to war with Japan. "Don't you think you'd better get confirmation first?" Winant asked. "Good God, you can't declare war on a radio announcement." Winant proposed a telephone call to the president.

"In two or three minutes Mr. Roosevelt came through. . . . 'It's quite true,' he said. 'They have attacked us at Pearl Harbour. We are all in the same boat now. . . . This certainly simplifies things. God be with you.' "

Harriman and Winant "took the shock with admirable fortitude," Churchill recalled. "In fact, one might almost have thought they had been delivered from a long pain."

"Fancy the U.S. Fleet being in harbour," the king wrote in his diary, "when the authorities must have known Japan was already on a war footing."

Churchill proceeded right away to see Roosevelt in Washington and was said to have changed for the better: "The Winston I knew in London frightened me," Lord Moran remembered. "I used to watch him as he went to his room with swift paces, the head thrust forward, scowling at the ground, the sombre countenance clouded, the features set and resolute, the jowl clamped down as if he had something between his teeth and did not mean to let go. I could see that he was carrying the weight of the world, and wondered how long he could go on like that." The trip to America rejuvenated him. Yet there, after opening a heavy White House window, he had a small heart attack. "There is nothing serious," Moran told him. "You have been overdoing things. . . . You're all right. Forget your damned heart."

The attack on Pearl Harbor had followed the invasion by Hitler's armies of the Soviet Union the previous summer. The Soviet Union and the United States were now fully at war. Churchill said with regard to the latter, "[P]reviously we were trying to seduce them. Now they are securely in the harem." More or less. The addition of two allies carried costs and burdens, as well as benefits. For all the matériel the Americans could provide, much would have to go to the Soviet Union, some no doubt at Britain's expense; for all the casualties the Soviets took, far exceeding those of the others combined, the moral and political demands their alliance would place upon Britain and the United States would be considerable. The Russians may have "look[ed] like a lot of pigstickers," according to Dill, but they counted. Coordination was not the least of the difficulties. The Allies needed a common strategy, and the challenge of reaching agreement about that, given vast differences in size, culture, and geography, was formidable. Churchill seemed to work for it harder than anyone. He traveled back and forth across the Atlantic, the Mediterranean, and the Urals. He was the man in the middle, sensitive to even the slightest (and sometimes not so slight) suggestion that the rulers of the two empires on the rise would gang up against the man leading the one on the ropes—the "Cinderella," in other words—"from Casablanca to Teheran, by way of Washington and Quebec," who "fought a series of rearguard actions for British influence, prestige and power." Churchill's chosen epithets were more rustic: "I will come anywhere, at any time, at any risk" despite being, as he put it, a "poor little English donkey" with the "great Russian bear on one side of me, with paws outstretched, and on the other side the great American buffalo." It was this poor donkey "who was the only one, the only one of the three, who knew the right way home." He would also describe the donkey as a lion and the buffalo as an elephant, but the point was the same.

The characterizations had more to do with the war than with personal politics. It was up to the Big Three to determine the general plan of the war, and this involved tough compromises. The centerpiece of the war from this point to the end of 1943 was fulfillment of the so-called Mediterranean strategy—securing command over North Africa and driving Italy out of the war, it was hoped, in order to divert sufficient Axis strength to the south so as to make victory on the eastern front more likely while preparing the way, eventually, for victory in the west. Neither Roosevelt nor Stalin was keen on the strategy, and it took all Churchill's talents of persuasion to drive it through. Stalin accused him of buying time in order to bleed Russians, no matter how well Churchill argued that the Mediterranean strategy would divert critical German strength—particularly aircraft—away from the Russian front. Roosevelt and his generals also protested, but on more theoretical grounds: if there was to be a cross-Channel invasion, it should happen soon. The Mediterranean flank, they said, was a policy of scatterization. It had long been American doctrine to "hit them where they are, not where they ain't." Halifax reiterated it in May 1943:

> The Americans want us to pledge ourselves to attack Northern France on a certain fixed date next year, whereas our people, while as anxious to do this as the Americans, feel that whether or not it will be a practicable operation depends on how hard we and the Russians can strain and hit the Germans between now and then. For this reason our people want to do everything to knock Italy out of the war.

Getting the Americans to accept that logic was exasperating. Churchill even went so far as to consider some strange alternatives in order to deflect pressure for the cross-Channel invasion—for example, another by way of Portugal and Spain. This produced even worse exasperation in Brooke: "Do you *know* the Pyrenees? I do. I've been all over those tracks as a boy. And if you think we're going to conduct the invasion of Europe across the Pyrenees, you're an even bigger fool than I thought you were!"

One of Churchill's least favorite Americanisms was "overall strategic concept." His riposte was to champion an "underall strategic concept." To him strategy was inseparable from experience and the long record of history. Marshall was not impressed: "I told him I was not interested in Drake and Frobisher, but I was interested in having a united front against Japan." Brooke, as usual, was torn:

> He knows no details, has only got half the picture in his mind, talks absurdities and makes my blood boil to listen to his nonsense. I find it hard to remain civil. And the wonderful thing is that ¾ of the population of the world imagine that Winston Churchill is one of the Strategists of History, a second Marlborough, and the other ¼ have no conception of what a public menace he is and has been throughout the war! It is far better that the world should never know, and never suspect the feet of clay of that otherwise superhuman being. Without him England was lost for a certainty, with him England has been on the verge of disaster time and again. . . . Never have I admired and despised a man simultaneously to the same extent. Never have such opposite extremes been combined in the same human being.

Internal—here understood as inter-Allied—obstacles once more compounded and complicated external ones. Sometimes it can be hard to say which were more trying for the protagonists. At the time the problems appeared in layers: fronts and more fronts, including the front of high expectations. Churchill in January "confess[ed] to feeling the weight of the war upon me even more than in the tremendous summer days of 1940." Lunching with the king on February 24, 1942, he said that "Burma, Ceylon, Calcutta, Madras and parts of Australia might well be lost." A week and a half later he added, "The weight of the war is very heavy now, and I must expect it to get steadily worse for some time to come." Brooke also admitted to having "had for the first time since the war started a growing conviction that we are going to lose this war unless we control it very differently and fight it with more determination."

Churchill had just survived a vote of no confidence in the Commons, which had made him "very angry," according to the king, like "hunting the tiger with angry wasps about him" from the ranks of his "weaker brethren." To him, it was an unnecessary, though not overly difficult, distraction at an inconvenient moment. The opposition to Churchill has tended to be minimized, even overlooked, in retrospect for obvious reasons, but it was there. It could have sidetracked and possibly overpowered him. Andrew Roberts has argued persuasively that the old Chamberlainites—still influential in framing Tory opinion—stood firmly in Churchill's way right up to the end of the war, in fact. "Churchill's position in the Conservative Party was never wholly free from ambiguity, and he was conscious of it."

A more minor but tiresome problem was the status of the Duke of Windsor. Relations between the two brothers had more or less frozen since the abdication, and the Windsors were left to do as they pleased so long as it was elsewhere. But the war threw up complications, not least because they had to leave France. In addition to coping with their obsession with money, keeping them away from

Britain was difficult once they had escaped. The governorship of the Bahamas became the compromise, one that the king fully supported. Halifax thought that "it is quite a good plan that they should go to the Bahamas . . . but I am sorry for the Bahamas." Chips Channon was another who thought the solution was for the best: "They will adore it, the petty pomp, the pretty Regency Government House, the beach and the bathing; and all the smart Americans will rush to Nassau to play backgammon with Wallis! It is an excellent appointment, and I suggested it two years ago and have been harping upon it ever since." He was not the only one. At one point later Lascelles, who never stopped mistrusting Churchill on this score, warned him to cease "harping on this problem" at the risk of the king's health.

The Windsors were not the only royals to worry him. Churchill quashed a parliamentary critic's attempt to see the appointment of the Duke of Gloucester, the king's mediocre younger brother, as commander in chief of the army, not an entirely ceremonial position. It was not the first time this duke would attempt to intervene in military matters—it was he, for example, who supposedly prompted the king to urge Chamberlain to dump the unpopular Leslie Hore-Belisha as secretary of state for war back in 1940. The rationale given now for this appointment was Churchill's being spread too thin and his meddling in military decisions, which seemed, by the beginning of 1942, to be contributing to bleak prospects. It would be better, Leo Amery said, if Churchill were both "Minister of Defence and P.M. only in name" so that his energies could be better focused on the war. Others were less certain. "Hitler may be a self-educated corporal and Winston may be an experienced student of tactics," noted Colville, "but unfortunately

Germany is organised as a war machine and England has only just realised the meaning of modern warfare." Yet "Hitler seems not only to direct the policy of war, he even plans the details."

"Yes," Churchill added, "that's just what I do."

The king's burden extended also to other royals whom he hosted or for whom he otherwise felt responsible. The best known was Queen Wilhelmina of the Netherlands, who arrived in Britain in the nick of time with little more than the clothes on her back. In the cases of others like Leopold of Belgium and Paul of Yugoslavia, the difficulties in their own countries also proved too great to surmount as each monarch's rule succumbed to desperation and defeat. The king may have recalled his father's experience with the Romanovs—George V had denied them sanctuary. He may have been determined to do better.

The war continued to go badly for Britain during the spring of 1942. In April came the so-called Baedeker Raids on cities, it was said, with more history than industry, like Exeter, Bath, Norwich, and York. The king met Marshall and Hopkins, and backed Brooke's proposed plan to attack German positions by way of Cyprus and Syria. This "resulted in good argument with Winston."

In June came the German recapture of Tobruk and with it Britain's fear of losing North Africa. Churchill was dismayed, in part because he got the news while he was again with Roosevelt in Washington. It brought the two closer together but was nonetheless "one of the heaviest blows I can recall during the war." Churchill added: "Defeat is one thing; disgrace is another." In response would come Operation Torch.

The invasion of North Africa presented several difficulties, not least of which was coordination with some unfamiliar and some-times disagreeable American allies. The above-mentioned saga of the second front need not be recounted here in full; suffice it to say that in addition to the Soviet element, which was paramount, there were persistent difficulties with the Americans. Since entering the war, they naturally demanded a heavier role in making strategic and operational decisions. Who would not have wanted to delay that moment as long as possible, if it was possible to delay at all?

Marshall, Hopkins, and now Admiral Ernest King had returned to London in July. "It will be a queer party," Brooke predicted, "as Harry Hopkins is for operating in Africa, Marshall wants to operate in Europe, and King is determined to strike in the Pacific!" Then there was the ever more demanding Stalin. That month the chiefs had told Churchill it was important "not [to] lead the Russians to think there is no chance of our attacking this year." Roberts has explained: "The double negative is instructive. Brooke did not want Stalin to know that there was no hope of a second front in Europe in 1942; however, he did not want the Americans to be told that Sledgehammer [the early plans for the invasion of France] was off the agenda 'at once.'" The war calculations were almost always zero-sum in this way. As the king later recorded in his diary: "[Churchill] has decided no more convoys to Russia are to be run due to the existing circumstances, which will allow the extra escorts for the Atlantic routes. He wants to tell Stalin the true reason for their stoppage, which is, that if we starve ourselves, we cannot help him with armaments." Churchill appealed directly to Stalin in person for patience, which he said "was like carrying a large lump of ice to the North Pole."

He flattered the Soviet leader's sense of *Realpolitik*. Often overlooked in Churchill's famous line about Russia being a riddle wrapped in a mystery inside an enigma is what he said next: "[B]ut perhaps there is a key. That key is Russian national interest." He drew for Stalin a picture of a crocodile, showing its soft belly and hard snout. Stalin liked this.

"If Torch succeeded," Stalin said, then "everybody will understand." But the Soviet leader was still seen to be unhappy. On the way back from Moscow, Wavell sat on the floor of the aircraft and wrote a ballad, which ended,

> *Prince of the Kremlin, here's a fond farewell,*
> *I've had to deal with many worse than you,*
> *You took it though you hated it like hell,*
> *No Second Front in 1942.*

The king welcomed Churchill back from his mission: "Your task was a very disagreeable one, but I congratulate you heartily on the skill with which you have accomplished it."

In addition to the turns in the war, the king was about to suffer a tough personal blow. His younger brother the Duke of Kent was killed in a plane crash a few days later on August 25. The king got the news while at Balmoral during dinner; when the others there saw his distress, everyone assumed Queen Mary had died, but instead it had been her favorite son.

Finally in November the luck all around changed. Churchill arrived for Tuesday luncheon on November 3 "carrying before him a red dispatch box." He said to the king, "I bring you victory." The queen "remember[ed] we looked at each other, and we thought, 'Is he going mad?' We had not heard that word since the war began."

Added the king: "A victory at last. How good it is for the nerves."
The Battle of El Alamein had been won.

This was the first major military victory since Churchill had
become prime minister. It came at just the right moment. The king
wrote to him enthusiastically:

> I must send you my warmest congratulations on the great
> Victory of the 8th Army in Egypt. I was overjoyed when I
> received the news & so was everybody else. In our many talks
> together over a long period I knew that the elimination of the
> Afrika Corps, the threat to Egypt, was your <u>one</u> aim, the most
> important of all the many other operations with which you
> have had to deal. When I look back & think of all the many
> arduous hours of work you have put in, & the many miles you
> have travelled, to bring this battle to such a successful con-
> clusion you have every right to rejoice; while the rest of our
> people will one day be very thankful to you for what you
> have done. I cannot say more. At last the Army has come into
> its own, as it is their victory primarily, ably helped by the
> forces of the air, & of those that work under the surface of
> the sea.
>
> I am so pleased that everybody is taking this victory in a
> quiet & thankful way, though their rejoicing is very deep &
> sincere.

Churchill replied:

> I am deeply grateful to Your Majesty for the most kind and
> gracious letter with which I have been honoured. I shall

always preserve it during the remaining years of my life, and it will remain as a record of the support and encouragement given by the Sovereign to his First Minister in good and dark days alike. No Minister in modern times, and I daresay in long past days, has received more help and comfort from the King, and this has brought us all thus far with broadening hopes and now I feel to brightening skies.

It is needless to me to assure Your Majesty of my devotion to Yourself and Family and to our ancient and cherished Monarchy—the true bulwark of British freedom against tyrannies of every kind; but I trust I may have the pleasure of feeling a sense of personal friendship which is very keen and lively in my heart and has grown strong in these hard times of war.

Some American servicemen attended a tea party at the palace for Thanksgiving. "One young officer, enjoying a whisky and soda, was heard to say, 'I never get Scotch at the White House. I like this king-racket.'" Roosevelt had written to the king that "on the whole the situation of all of us is better . . . and that, while 1943 will not see a complete victory for us, things are on the up-grade." The new year, 1943, thus began on an optimistic note. Brooke could not

help glancing back at Jan 1st last year when I could see nothing but calamities ahead. . . .

Horrible doubts, horrible nightmares, which grew larger and larger as the days went on till it felt as if the whole Empire was collapsing round my head. . . . And now! We start 1943 under conditions I would never have dared to hope. Russia has held, Egypt for the present is safe. There is a hope of clearing North Africa of Germans in the near future. The Mediterranean may be partially opened. Malta is safe for the present. We can now work freely against Italy, and Russia is scoring wonderful successes in Southern Russia. We are certain to have many setbacks to face, many troubles, and many shattered hopes, but for all that the horizon is infinitely brighter.

The king continued to worry. "Outwardly one has to be optimistic about the future in 1943, but inwardly I am depressed at the present prospect."

Churchill headed to North Africa in January. He nearly froze during the journey after ordering the heat on his airplane shut off on account of the fumes. Perhaps this was a source of his illness the following month. He developed what may have been his worst-ever case of pneumonia—or it may have been revenge for the style of his journey. Brooke saw him in Marrakesh, for example:

It was all I could do to remain serious. The room . . . was done up in Moorish style, the ceiling was a marvelous fresco of green, blue and gold. The head of the bed rested in an alcove of Moroccan design with a religious light shining on either side, the bed was covered in a blue silk covering with a 6 in[ch] wide lace "entre deux" and the rest of the room in harmony with the Arabic ceiling. And there in the bed was Winston in his green, red and gold dragon dressing gown, his hair, or what there was of it, standing on end, the religious lights shining on his cheeks, and a large cigar in his face!!

Edward Spears has recalled a similar "apparition" from one of their earlier visits to France: it "resembled an angry Japanese genie, in long, flowing red silk kimono over other similar but white garments, girdled with a white belt of like material, [and] stood there, sparse hair on end, and said with every sign of anger: '*Uh ay ma bain?*'"

"I suppose I ought to have said, '*Uh ay MONG bain?*'" Churchill later corrected. He liked ruses, costumes, and disguises, though they made him look like "a figure which might have stepped straight from the world of Walt Disney." At Casablanca his code name was Mr. P; Roosevelt's was Admiral Q. "We must mind our Ps and Qs." The king may have agreed. He sent an anxious letter on February 22:

My dear Winston,

I am very sorry to hear that you are ill, & I hope that you will soon be well again. But do please take this opportunity for a rest . . . you must get back your strength for the strenuous coming months. I missed being able to have a talk to you last Tuesday, & I understand we may not meet next Tuesday either, so I am writing to you instead.

I do not feel at all happy about the present political situation in North Africa. I know we had to leave the political side of Torch to the Americans, while we were able to keep Spain & Portugal friendly during the time the operation was going on. Since then I feel the underhand dealings of Murphy with the French in North Africa, & his contacts with Vichy have placed both America & this country in an invidious position. I know we had to tread warily at the start, but is there nothing we can do now to strengthen Macmillan's & Alexander's hands in both the political and military sphere, to make the French sides come together. . . .

I should not think of bothering you with these questions at this moment, but I do feel worried about them, & I would like an assurance from you that they are being carefully watched.

I cannot discuss these vital matters with anyone but yourself.

Churchill's seven-page-long reply came from his sickbed, where he lay with a temperature of 102 degrees:

I do not feel seriously disturbed by the course of events in North Africa, either political or even military although naturally there is much about both aspects which I would rather have different. . . . It is quite true that we have for this purpose and to safeguard our vital communications, to work with a mass of French officials who were appointed by Vichy; but without them I really do not know how the country could be governed. . . . The irruption of de Gaulle or his agents into this field, especially if forcibly introduced by us, would cause nothing but trouble. . . . It is entirely his fault that a good arrangement was not made between the two French factions. . . . Although I have been hampered by high fever from reading all the telegrams, I think I have the picture truly in my mind, and I wish indeed that I could have given this account to Your Majesty verbally at luncheon.

The king decided not to pursue the matter further, at least not in writing. He confided in his diary: "[T]he P.M. . . . assured me that the N. Afn. Situation was going well. . . . We had to use the French who were there. . . . The Americans will learn through defeat, & the Germans will learn from the 8th Army when they meet in Tunisia."

On March 23 they resumed their weekly luncheons. Two weeks later Churchill predicted that there would be more success to come. The "Axis," he said, is "having a 'Bumkirk' in Tunisia." General Alexander had already reported: "The orders you gave me on August 10 1942 have been fulfilled. His Majesty's enemies, together with their impedimenta, have been completely eliminated from Egypt, Cyrenaica, Libya, and Tripolitania. I now await your further instructions." The German and Italian forces there surrendered in May. "It is an overwhelming victory," wrote the king:

> I wish to tell you how profoundly I appreciate the fact that its initial conception and successful prosecution are largely due to your vision and to your unflinching determination in the face of early difficulties. The African campaign has immeasurably increased the debt that this country, and indeed all the United Nations, owe to you.

Churchill replied:

> No Minister of the Crown has ever received more kindness and confidence from his Sovereign than I have done. . . . This has been a precious aid and comfort to me. . . . My father and my grandfather both served in Cabinets of Queen Victoria's reign, and I myself have been a Minister under your Majesty's grandfather, your father, and your self for many years.

The signal compliment which your Majesty has paid me on this occasion goes far beyond my deserts but will remain as a source of lively pleasure to me as long as I live.

The king's telegram to Churchill on this occasion was publicized widely. By May the prime minister was back in Washington. Halifax said, "I have never seen him in better heart or form . . . an amazing contrast to the very tired and nerve-strained PM I saw last August in England."

The king meanwhile suggested that he pay a visit to the troops in North Africa. Churchill agreed that this was a good idea. So, traveling as "General Lyon" (later he would prefer "General Collingwood"), the king went on his first visit to the army overseas since he had inspected the BEF in France in 1939. He rode in a large Ford that flew the royal standard. Some sang "For He's a Jolly Good Fellow" and gave him ovations. He proceeded on to Malta, where the residents hung "rugs and carpets and curtains . . . out of the windows—anything to make a show." There were so many flowers thrown at him, parts of his white uniform became a multicolored palette. He said he was "the happiest man in Malta today."

The next venture was the conquest of Italy. It proved to be much harder and bloodier than most people had expected. As Churchill had once said about a planned attack on Burma: "You might as well eat a porcupine one quill at a time," and that could also have applied here. The idea was first to take Sicily, then the whole of Italy. His reaction to the American proposal to begin with a more digestible portion—Sardinia, for example—was negative: "I absolutely refuse to be fobbed off with a sardine." North Africa must act "as a 'springboard,' not as a 'sofa' to future action."

The invasion in Sicily began in July and led to the fall of Mussolini. It produced more confusion than outright jubilation. The Allies then fought their way up the country, over and through some of the most difficult, mountainous terrain in Europe. These obstacles were compounded by the ambiguous aspect of Italian partisanship, for it was unclear sometimes who was fighting whom. The Soviets' mood continued to fester. The Italian struggle prolonged the opening of the second front that Stalin had constantly urged. Churchill did what he could to mitigate the problem, or at least it appeared that way. Brooke regarded this approach to have been "wrong from the very start. . . . We have bowed and scraped to them, done all we could for them and never asked them for a single fact or figure concerning their production, strength, dispositions etc. As a result they despise us and have no use for us except for what they can get out of us."

At this moment the king, at the suggestion of the Foreign Office, approved a gift from the British people to the Soviet defenders of Stalingrad in the form of a large sword, called the Sword of Stalingrad. Churchill would present it to Stalin at Tehran for the first of the Big Three conferences in November 1943. The king seemed to be pleased with the sword when he saw it, though he merely noted the absence of a date and asked how much it cost. The sword went on tour across England, where large crowds of people waited to see it. Lascelles managed to prevent the king from having it ornamented with bears by informing him that the Russian bear was generally used "by foreign cartoonists . . . to give [Stalin] a sword with bears on it would be like giving the French one ornamented with frogs." Churchill handed the sword to Stalin in a special ceremony when they met at Tehran. Stalin kissed the sword, said a few gracious words of thanks, and then handed it to Marshal Voroshilov, who dropped it on his toe.

At Tehran, Churchill also praised Roosevelt for preventing "a revolutionary upheaval in the United States in 1933." He said Stalin "would be ranked with the great heroes of Russian history and had earned the title 'Stalin the Great.'" He then declared, "I drink to the Proletarian masses."

Stalin responded, "I drink to the Conservative Party."

Next they were treated to a bit of entertainment that recalled one of Churchill's favorite words: imperturbable.

Stalin's interpreter, Pavlov, had become the victim of a clumsy waiter carrying "an enormous ice-cream perched on a large block of ice in which there burned a candle." The man's eyes seemed to be "popping as he looked at Stalin and not the way he was going. . . . He allowed it to tilt more and more dangerously. . . . The guests sat transfixed, trying to guess where it would fall . . . and by the time he reached Pavlov . . . the laws of gravity could be denied no longer and the pudding descended like an avalanche on his unfortunate head. In a moment ice-cream was oozing out of his hair, his ears, his shirt and even his shoes. But his translation never checked."

The results of Tehran were otherwise mixed. Stalin and Churchill had argued badly over the cross-Channel invasion and other subjects. Churchill got little support from Roosevelt. He felt more and more isolated, "appalled by his own impotence." The Americans seemed wedded to an invasion taking place during the next six months. Dill took a sober view, having written to Brooke in October: "I do not believe that it was ever possible to make the Americans more Mediterranean-minded than they are today. The

American Chiefs of Staff have given way to our views a thousand times more than we have given way to theirs."

But he added: "P.S. Winston is the most popular foreigner America has ever known, & his influence is great. But there is a grave danger that, with anti-F.D.R. propaganda & perhaps one or two ill-advised remarks by W.S.C., the cry may go up that he is trying to run America as well as Britain." That risk remained. But the threat of defeat appeared to have passed.

The king in his Christmas broadcast repeated the note of optimism with which the year had begun. He reminded his countrymen that they ought "not rest from our task until it is nobly ended. Meanwhile within these islands, we have tried to be worthy of our fathers; we have tried to carry into the dawn the steadfastness and courage vouchsafed to us when we stood alone in the darkness." Hiding in a remote part of the Apennines in Italy, the fugitive soldier Eric Newby heard it on the radio following

> a great lunch . . . to the accompaniment of awful whistlings and other atmospherics, [then] the laboured but sincere-sounding voice of the King speaking from Sandringham. . . . "Some of you may hear me in your aircraft, in the jungles of the Pacific or on the Italian Peaks. . . . Wherever you may be your thoughts will be in distant places and your hearts with those you love."

This had an effect on Newby and his fellow fugitive, "with all the food we had eaten and the wine we had drunk, and the people in the room witnessed the awful spectacle, something which they are unlikely ever to see again, of two Englishmen with tears running down their cheeks."

The broadcasts evidently had an important function beyond reinstilling faith in the monarchy. "Anyway," Lascelles has written, "if the foundations are in process of disintegration, the process will not be arrested by turgid royal broadcasts.... Our 'levelling' process will doubtless follow a steeper gradient ... but I don't believe it will ever become a precipice." Some may have turned away from the monarchy. It would not last forever, Lascelles wrote, but "at the moment I believe it rests on foundations as durable as it ever had." The king and his country would fight on.

CHAPTER TEN

Victory

Nineteen forty-four: General Brooke visited Sandringham in January. He and his companion found the house empty and were directed to a smaller one nearby.

At the gate we were stopped by a policeman who after examining our identities turned on a series of little magic blue lights on either side of the avenue up to the house. . . . [In] the drawing room . . . I found the Queen alone with the two princesses. . . . The older of the two princesses also came along to assist in entertaining me, whilst the younger one remained on the sofa reading *Punches* and emitting ripples of giggles and laughter at the jokes.

He met the king privately and observed that he "displays the greatest interest and is evidently taking the greatest trouble to keep himself abreast of everything." After a couple of days he concluded:

It has been a most interesting experience, and one which has greatly impressed me. The one main impression that I have carried away with me is that the King, Queen and their two daughters provide one of the very best examples of English family life. A thoroughly closely knit and happy family all wrapped up in each other. Secondly I was greatly impressed by the wonderful atmosphere entirely devoid of all pomposity, stiffness or awkwardness.

———

Churchill was less cheerful. "[T]his world ('this dusty and lamentable ball') is now too beastly to live in. People act so revoltingly that they just don't deserve to survive." On March 14 he and the king had been dining at Number 10 when the air-raid warning sounded, and all went down to the shelter. Churchill "kept dodging out and coming back to say no one must move." But the king was "in terrific form—obviously enjoying himself to the limit—and very animated."

A week later they heard the report of the queen's brother, David Bowes-Lyon, who was posted in Washington with the Political Warfare Executive, Britain's Washington spy post (whose name, incidentally, he was said to have invented). "Anglo-American relations," he estimated, "had now reached their lowest level. . . . The reasons for this were not caused by any incidents, nor were they a temporary slump caused by election tactics. The reason was fundamental: the Americans now realised their immense power."

With the Americans as allies, the asymmetry of this alliance had become more evident, and only appeared to grow. "The British had pushed the world round for the last hundred years and now the Americans were going to do it," he added, and "we crawl too much to the Americans. Recent telegrams of the P.M. to F.D.R. have been almost nauseating in their sentimental and subservient flattery." Churchill, however, continued to insist on making the alliance work, even if it meant more policy sacrifices. Despite the "lot of fretfulness," as Churchill had characterized similar talks to the king back in August 1943, everything would be all right.

By May of the following year, collaboration had begun to pay off. Brooke felt he could "[t]hank heaven the Italian attack is going well . . . we have proved Marshall and the American Chiefs of Staff were all wrong arguing that the Italians would retire before we could attack them. . . . First Stalingrad . . . secondly Tunisia . . . thirdly the Dnieper River Bend." Churchill later called this moment the war's "supreme climax," the point at which victory became a question of timing. The Allies controlled the Mediterranean, half of Italy, and a renewed eastern front. Now was the moment to set "the keystone of the arch of Anglo-American co-operation," the long-awaited invasion of France: Operation Overlord. Some people had expressed reservations. One was Field Marshal Jan Christian Smuts. "Slim Jan," the South African premier, was also known as Churchill's "surrogate uncle" whose "mind moved majestically amid the vagaries of Fortune." Smuts was an old adversary in the Boer War who had nevertheless helped to spare his life. He was now one of the tiny handful to whom Churchill listened almost unconditionally.

Smuts shared his concerns over the timing and viability of the operation with the king, whose concurrence was noted back in October: "Smuts is not happy about 'Overlord' & is doing his best to convince Winston that we must go on with W's own strategy of attacking the 'under belly' of the Axis." He "agree[d] with S. about all this. If you have a good thing stick to it."

The king repeated this in a letter to Churchill and proposed that the three of them meet over dinner with the likely expectation that, as per custom, "old Smuts, sitting like an owl on its perch, would hop down and play an always predominant part." Churchill sent a tart reply accepting the invitation, adding, "There is no possibility of our going back on what is agreed. Both the U.S. Staff and Stalin would violently disagree with us." The three worked through their misgivings and reached a consensus. Their meeting served to confirm Churchill's position but also the king's and Smuts's priority: "that Italy has got to be secured at all costs, before Overlord."

Churchill had told Brooke that he wanted him to command the invasion. He reneged after Roosevelt pushed hard for Marshall, only to change his mind in favor of Eisenhower—a crushing blow to Brooke, who told Churchill, simply, that he was "disappointed." In January 1944, Eisenhower arrived and drew a sketch of the Overlord plan for the king. This was followed, in May, by a full preview. It was the anniversary of the coronation, but the king insisted the regalia not be on display. Lascelles was apt, quoting William Pitt the Younger: "This is neither a fit time nor a proper subject for the exhibition of a gaudy fancy or the wanton blandishments of theatrical enchantment."

The king, Smuts, Churchill, and the various commanders gathered at headquarters, which was then located in St. Paul's School. Churchill, in his greatcoat, and the king sat in armchairs, while everyone else sat at school desks facing a large map set up on the stage. Eisenhower began the briefings, followed by several other commanders, the best of which was given, Ismay said, by Montgomery—St. Paul's had been his school, after all. At the end, the king spoke without notes. Exactly what he said is not recorded, but in the archives there is this draft:

> I have known of the existence of this Operation ever since it was first mooted and I have followed all its preparations very carefully. I have heard and seen reports from my P.M. as Minr. of Defence, & from the Supreme Comdr. . . .
>
> This is the biggest Combined Operation ever thought out in the world. But it is much more than this. It is a Combined Opn. of 2 Countries, the United States & British Empire. As I look around this audience of British & Americans I can see that you have equally taken a part in its preparation. I wish you all success & with God's help you will succeed.

"Thus all was arranged," according to Churchill, "and the march which had begun at Lake Chad ended through Paris at Berchtesgaden."

There would be more obstacles to overcome before that, but there now arose one that few had anticipated, at least in its intensity.

> When I attended my weekly luncheon with the King on Tuesday, May 30, His Majesty asked me where I intended to be on D Day.
>
> I replied that I proposed to witness the bombardment from one of the cruiser squadrons. His Majesty immediately said he would like to come too. He had not been under fire

except in air raids since the Battle of Jutland, and eagerly welcomed the prospect of renewing the experiences of his youth.

Churchill was sympathetic. "What fun," he said, "to land with the troops on D-Day and perhaps get there ahead of Monty!"

This became perhaps the only serious break between the two in the course of the war. In the king's version, as recorded in his diary, he "asked W. where he would be on D day or rather the night before & he told me glibly he hoped to see the initial attack from one of the bombarding ships. I was not surprised & when I suggested that I should go as well (the idea has been in my mind for some time) he reacted well."

When Lascelles got wind of the idea, he did not take it seriously. Then he panicked. He told the king that "His Majesty's anxieties would be increased if he heard his Prime Minister was at the bottom of the English Channel" and insisted he dissuade Churchill from succumbing to such "sheer selfishness, plus vanity." The king then sent the following letter:

My dear Winston,

I have been thinking a great deal of our conversation yesterday, and I have come to the conclusion that it would not be right for either you or I to be where we planned to be on D Day. I don't think I need emphasise what it would mean to me personally, and to the whole Allied cause, if at this juncture a chance bomb, torpedo, or even a mine, should remove you from the scene; equally a change of Sovereign at this moment would be a serious matter for the country and Empire. We should both, I know, love to be there, but in all seriousness I would ask you to reconsider your plan. Our presence, I feel, would be an embarrassment to those responsible for fighting the ship or ships in which we were, despite anything we might say to them.

So, as I said, I have very reluctantly come to the conclusion that the right thing to do is what normally falls to those at the top on such occasions, namely, to remain at home and wait.

As Stamfordham had once instructed King George V, "It [is] the duty of a constitutional monarch to *act* on his Prime Minister's advice but not to *make promises*." The king therefore chose an appeal to Churchill's friendship over his office. Churchill did not see matters that way. He responded that as minister of defense he had a duty to observe the invasion in person and that the risk to him was small in any event. Lascelles took a similar line, in reverse, namely that Churchill, like any minister, needed the king's permission to travel abroad, to which Churchill replied that he would be on board a British navy ship the entire time, and therefore did not need permission. Lascelles said the ship would travel beyond British territorial waters. And so it went. Finally, the king wrote to Churchill:

I want to make one more appeal to you not to go to sea on D Day. Please consider my own position. I am a younger man than you, I am a sailor, and as King I am the head of all these Services. There is nothing I would like better than to go to sea, but I have agreed to stay at home; is it fair that you should then do exactly what I should have liked to do myself? You said yesterday afternoon that it would be a fine thing for the King to lead his troops into battle, as in old days; if the King cannot do this, it does not seem to me right that his Prime Minister should take his place. . . . I ask you most earnestly to consider the whole question again, and not let your personal wishes, which I very well understand, lead you to depart from your own high standard of duty to the State.

Lascelles threatened to involve Smuts, and the king even suggested he drive personally to Portsmouth to prevent Churchill from boarding ship. Neither proved necessary. After some delay and with more than a little annoyance, Churchill backed down. His explanation and his tone are noteworthy, for this was the only time during the course of the war that the king succeeded in countermanding one of his wishes outright.

Sir, I cannot really feel that the first paragraph of your letter takes sufficient account of the fact that there is absolutely no comparison in the British Constitution between a Sovereign and a subject. If Your Majesty had gone, as you desire, on board one of your ships in this bombarding action it would have required the Cabinet approval beforehand. . . . On the other hand, as Prime Minister and Minister of Defence I ought to be allowed to go where I consider it necessary to the discharge of my duty. . . . I rely on my own judgment, invoked in many serious matters, as to what are the proper limits of risk which a person who discharges my duties is entitled to run. I must most earnestly ask Your Majesty that no principle shall be laid down which inhibits my freedom of movement when I judge it necessary to acquaint myself with conditions in the various theatres of war. Since Your Majesty does me the honour to be so much concerned about my personal safety on this occasion, I must defer to Your Majesty's wishes, and indeed commands. It is a great comfort to me to know that they arise from Your Majesty's desire to continue me in your service. Though I regret that I cannot go, I am deeply grateful to Your Majesty for the motives which have guided Your Majesty in respect of

Your Majesty's humble and devoted servant and subject.

So came D-Day, the "sixth hour of the sixth day of the sixth month" of 1944. Churchill entered the House of Commons to speak to the members, who had been waiting anxiously for him to arrive. They cheered when they saw him, and again when he asked them to recognize the liberation of Rome. He then proceeded to inform them that "an immense armada of upwards of 4,000 ships, together with several thousand smaller craft, crossed the Channel." He told them of the landings by air and by sea, on the beaches and behind enemy lines. He then reported that "[t]he fire of the shore batteries has been largely quelled. . . . So far the Commanders who are engaged report that everything is proceeding according to plan. And what a plan!" The king broadcast at 9:00 p.m.:

Four years ago, our Nation and Empire stood alone against an overwhelming enemy, with our backs to the wall. Tested as never before in our history, in God's providence we survived the test; the spirit of the people, resolute, dedicated, burned like a bright flame, lit surely from those Unseen Fires which nothing can quench.

Marshall, General Hap Arnold, Smuts, and the British chiefs of staff visited the king for an after-action report that lasted, thanks to Churchill's verbosity, until 2:00 a.m. He had resigned himself to watching the departing troops from port. A few days later, he would be allowed to visit them. "How I wish you were here!" he wrote to Roosevelt after having ridden in a torpedo boat and singing "Rule Britannia" with some officers. He "had a jolly day on Monday on the beaches and inland. . . . After doing much laborious duty we went and had a plug at the Hun from our destroyer, but although the range was 6,000 yards he did not honour us with a reply." The king followed, sailing across the Channel amid the dense traffic, and then was greeted in France by General Montgomery. "It was most encouraging to know that it was possible for me to land on the beaches only 10 days after D Day." He was seen to be extremely happy. "If 'Action Stations' had been ordered, he would have been happier still."

The moment could not be relished for long. The Germans had begun a new air assault, only now with the dreaded V-1 rockets, the so-called doodlebugs. They caught many people by surprise; even Lord Cherwell did not believe how destructive they could be. "For sheer damnable devilry what could be worse than this awful instrument?" asked an enraged James Lees-Milne. The V-2s, introduced a short while later, were supposedly more powerful but less terrifying, "for when you hear them you know you're all right." The attacks hit, as before, close to home. The Guards Chapel at Wellington

Barracks was destroyed; the king and Churchill retreated once more to the palace air-raid shelter for their luncheons. Lees-Milne and others resumed their duty as wardens and stretcher-bearers. Harold Nicolson's had been to sit "on the top of the Victoria Tower pressing bells." To him it was "immensely exciting."

Churchill traveled to Moscow again in October. He and Stalin went to the Bolshoi, where they were feted by crowds. The experience was replicated the following month in Paris when he and Eden joined Charles de Gaulle at the Hôtel de Ville: the city had been liberated in August. Churchill was given a German flag and invited to speak in his funny French. He and de Gaulle went on parade, laid a wreath at the Arc de Triomphe, at the Clemenceau statue, and at Foch's tomb; he was awarded the Croix de la Libération. The crowds chanted "Chur-chill!" and, according to Eden, "not for one minute did Winston stop crying . . . he could have filled buckets." De Gaulle had given him the room at the Quai d'Orsay that the king and queen had used on their last visit before the war. Eden went to see him and heard sounds in the bathroom: "Come in, come in, that is if you can bear to see me in a gold bath when you only have a silver one," Churchill announced. The bathtub had been meant for Goering.

"Do you think that there is any chance of London being 'Liberated' in the coming months?" the queen asked Churchill. "My heart aches for our wonderful brave people . . . and I long for them to have a lightening of their burden." They were almost there.

In February 1945 came the conference at Yalta. Churchill arrived in his Skymaster; FDR in his, called the *Sacred Cow*. Everything they could ask for was provided, even when the requests were made in jest. When Churchill noted that FDR's orange tree provided more fruit than his, a new one appeared right away, along with lemon trees, "gold fish in a stone pool brought from who knows where . . . [and] flower beds bright with zinnias and geraniums, blooming hypocritically in their buried pots."

They ate and drank well. But Churchill was "fiercely controversial." By now, he was playing a losing hand against the Soviet Union, and the ailing Roosevelt seemed unable to help. So much time had passed since Churchill promised, back in 1940, that a liberated Poland would rejoin the European family of nations. It was now self-evident that "all the Balkans, except Greece, are going to be Bolshevised; and there is nothing I can do to prevent it. There is nothing I can do for poor Poland either." Still, he said a month later that he had "not the slightest intention of being cheated over Poland, not even if we go to the verge of war with Russia," but there was precious little leverage. Stalin took little time to reveal his policy. Churchill was with the king at Buckingham Palace on February 28 when news arrived of the first Soviet heavy-handedness toward Romania and Bulgaria. "My God," Eden said, "what a mess Europe is in! What a mess!" Indeed, Stalin in Eden's recollection was "the only one of the three who has a clear view of what he wants and is a tough negotiator. PM is all emotion in these matters, FDR vague and jealous of others."

In March, Colville noticed "[i]t was strange to see footmen in livery again" at embassy dinner parties. The next month the sky was "black with Fortresses and Liberators" coming home from their bombing missions across the Channel, where earlier "the Battle of Britain raged hottest and the Flying Bombs did their worst." Churchill visited the Rhine, and Brooke feared that "he longed to get into the most exposed position possible . . . at this moment of success. He had often told me that the way to die is to pass out fighting when your blood is up and you feel nothing." He would live, but in a few weeks Roosevelt died. The king discouraged Churchill from attending the funeral in the United States and instead they took part in a memorial service in the damaged St. Paul's Cathedral on April 17. The king and Princess Elizabeth wore their military uniforms—his naval and hers from the Auxiliary Territorial Service. The queen dressed in black. "The Star-Spangled Banner" was played and Churchill cried, conspicuously.

Lascelles, meanwhile, had ordered floodlights at Buckingham Palace be prepared for an anticipated royal appearance on the balcony. It was rumored to be unsafe and in need of reinforcement, and the king wondered about "the dramatic conclusion to the war and to his reign if it disintegrated under the weight of himself, the Queen and Churchill."

Then, victory.

Ismay was the one to give Churchill the news. Or almost. Eisenhower called Ismay at 3:00 a.m. and told it to him. When Ismay then put a call in to Churchill, his line failed, so "[t]here was nothing for it but to collect some coppers, put on a dressing-gown, and go to the public call-box a hundred yards down the road," only to be told that Churchill had somehow "already heard the glad news and gone to bed."

Churchill later called the king and told him, then celebrated with his staff.

Brooke merely noted that his "main sensation is one of infinite mental weariness!" The king also was said to have "felt the strain of the war terribly. He looked shattered." Churchill had been exhausted for weeks, often staying in bed and working from there throughout the day. On V-E Day he roused himself to attend or preside at commemorations lasting well until the early hours of the morning.

He drafted the last paragraph of the king's victory broadcast, ending with the line "The power and might of Germany is finally broken." The king had to wait another day to make it, since V-E Day was to be declared on May 8, 1945. It was one of the few times in his life that he genuinely seemed eager to speak by radio, "just like waiting for one's wife to have a baby." In spite of gathering crowds at the palace, the king resisted showing himself on the balcony, "not wishing to shoot his grouse before the Twelfth, so to speak."

The next day was, appropriately, a Tuesday. The king recorded: "The Prime Minister came to lunch. We congratulated each other on the end of the European War. The day we have been longing for has arrived at last, & we can look back with thankfulness to God that our tribulation is over." Trafalgar Square had filled with people. All the surrounding streets were full of bodies pressing to be near the palace. Loudspeakers had been set up near Parliament Square, and from them came Churchill's voice, following the chimes of Big Ben. His words echoed off the walls of the palace. He announced the German surrender, after which "God Save the King" was sung.

James Lees-Milne wandered to Piccadilly Circus, which was lit up by bright lamps. The crowd danced and sang and laughed. The people "were orderly and good humoured. All the English virtues were on the surface.... The scene was more Elizabethan than neo-Georgian, a spontaneous peasant game, a dance round the maypole, almost Bruegelian, infinitely bucolic." The two princesses ran around the streets, as incognito as possible. Back at the palace, Their Majesties appeared on the balcony, over and over. Churchill joined them. "One's heart was too full with all the cheering and recollections of six years to speak to anyone," Halifax wrote. "It is an amazing thing that just as both Houses go to the place of worship, so the populace flocks to Buckingham Palace to see the symbol of everything that they instinctively gather up in articulate patriotism."

On May 17 the king delivered his victory address to Parliament. He delivered it flawlessly except for a slip on the word "imperishable" and a breaking of his voice when he mentioned the Duke of Kent.

A reprise took place in August with V-J Day. Crowds swarmed, facing the crimson-and-gold-decked balcony of Buckingham Palace, chanting, "We want the King. We want the Queen," although less raucously than before. The "façade looked splendid, but the minute royal standard was out of scale." Then, as Lees-Milne observed,

[a]t last, just after midnight, the French window opened a crack, then wider, and out came the King and Queen. They were tiny . . . her little figure swathed in a fur, and something sparkling in her hair. The gold buttons of his Admiral's uniform glistened. Both waved in a slightly self-conscious fashion and stood for three minutes. Then they retreated. The crowd waved with great applause, and all walked quietly home.

"Thus has ended the World War which started 6 years ago to-day," wrote the king in his diary on September 3.

One evening the previous May, Lascelles had noticed an owl sitting and hooting on top of one of the chimney pots at Windsor. "I've never seen an owl do this before." The country's mood had shifted. In July, Churchill took a restful visit to France, where he began to paint again. He went on to Berlin, where he toured the Chancellery building, whose floors were covered with "files, papers, pieces of broken furniture . . . [and] hundreds of new Iron Cross medals," and Hitler's bunker. Churchill "said nothing. He did not seem greatly interested. . . . His thoughts were elsewhere."

Denouement

I shall be glad when this election business is over," Churchill had said. "It hovers over me like a vulture of uncertainty in the sky." He did not like elections but had waged them most of his life. He liked to quote his father in this respect: "Never . . . be afraid of British democracy." But it disappointed him. Some people threw stones; a squib nearly hit him in the face. And he was exhausted—more so, he said, than he had ever been since the Boer War.

On Election Day, July 26, 1945, Churchill was seen in his siren suit holding a cigar. He appeared impassive; the only emotion he showed was when he was told that the king had sent word to say how much he would be missed. The British people had defeated his party and turned him out of office.

"Five million against us."

"Keep alert," he advised some young friends of one of his daughters. "It's *your* turn now. I've thrown the reins on the horse's neck. . . ."

"But you won the race, sir," one of them interjected.

"Yes . . . and in consequence I've been warned off the Turf!"

Beaverbrook had predicted the result: "Winston is a great war P.M., but he is *not* the man for the peace." Or as Churchill put it, he would not be the one to "bring the magic of averages to the aid of millions," and would not even be on hand through the end of the Potsdam Conference—code-named "Terminal." He was replaced there by Clement Attlee.

It is not difficult to imagine how he must have felt. He had given a sense of it, some decades earlier, in a biographical sketch of King Alfonso XIII of Spain. In it he made a distinction between monarchs and politicians, noting that the latter should be prepared to be tossed out at any time, but if this happened to the former, the damage was spiritual as well as political. For him at this moment, though, the two roles and sets of emotions must have blurred. Poor Alfonso: "To begin life again in middle age under novel and contracted conditions with a status and in a state of mind never before experienced. . . . Surely a harsh destiny!" Now the portrayal came closer to home: "To have given his best, to have faced every peril and anxiety, to have accomplished great things, to have presided over his country during all the perils of the twentieth century . . . and then to be violently rejected by the nation of which he was so proud, of whose tradition and history he was the embodiment, the nation he had sought to represent in all the finest actions of his life—surely this was enough to try the soul of mortal man." Even, or especially, if he were warned to expect it.

Maybe his defeat would turn out, to repeat his familiar riposte, to be another blessing in disguise, "quite effectively disguised," but for now he felt right back in 1922 and all the other dark times: rejected and rebuffed.

On July 30 "at 7 p.m. he said quaintly to [Captain] Pim: 'Fetch me my carriage and I shall go to the Palace.'" There he submitted his resignation. The king recorded that "it was a very sad meeting."

> I told him I thought the people were very ungrateful after the way they had been led in the War. He was very calm. . . . I asked him if I should send for Mr. Attlee to form a government & he agreed. We said good bye & I thanked him for all his help to me during the 5 War Years.

The next day he wrote:

> Your breadth of vision & your grasp of the essential things were a great comfort to me in the darkest days of the War, & I like to think that we have never disagreed on any really important matter. For all those things I thank you most sincerely. I feel that your conduct as Prime Minister & Minister of Defence has never been surpassed. You have had many difficulties to deal with both as a politician & as a strategist of war but you have always surmounted them with supreme courage.

The king's point is well taken. There were few recorded disagreements between the two, apart from the rather silly D-Day affair. Where the king found Churchill's logic wanting, he generally asked for more information or for a clarification, that is, to be persuaded, which he almost always was with a bit of his own contribution. The lack of disagreement may be taken as resulting from deference to Churchill, but it was not doctrinaire.

So, in the end—did the king matter to the war? Operationally, probably not. There is not a single major decision or policy that Churchill and his government changed solely on his advice or only to satisfy him. He was no hidden hand, nor sought to be one. But the operational question is the wrong one; it does not solve the puzzle posed at the outset of this book. A better conclusion is found by asking whether their alliance mattered for Churchill and his own capacity as leader. Here the answer must be yes. It had as much to do with the character of the king as it did with the deficiencies of Churchill, if that's what they were. No matter how much he was in demand in the spring of 1940, Churchill was regarded in some critical corners of British society as something of a foreign body: he was mistrusted and always would be, not merely for who he was but also for what he did over the course of his turbulent political career.

The king augmented Churchill's authority and, in a curious way, contributed an aspect of humility that he otherwise would have found difficult to feign, especially among the classes that were coolest toward him. It underwrote Churchill's sense of prerogative and gave him a freer hand to cast himself as his nation's selfless savior. This might have happened anyway, Britain being as desperate as she was at the time and Churchill being so indomitable. However, after reconstructing the history of the two men in tandem it becomes very difficult to imagine Churchill succeeding in that without the full support of the king, and certainly not if the two had worked deliberately at cross purposes. This was the outer gift. The inner one has already been discussed—that is, the degree to which the two men helped to clarify each other's thinking and strengthen each other's spirit through the exercise of a professional and personal alliance against multiple adversaries, including their own fears and deficiencies. This is their primary lesson for leadership: it must have the capacity to work in combination and in concert, or it will not work at all. Prerogative, like adversity, has a fungible value. Anchor it too firmly in one person and it will almost certainly obstruct and destroy him.

"[I]s it true," Churchill's young grandson Nicholas Soames once asked, "that you are the greatest man in the world?" "Yes," came the reply, "and now bugger off." Roy Jenkins, who has related that story, agreed. At the very end of his long biography of Churchill, the last book he would ever write, he concluded:

> Of more importance than a comparison of the different obse-
> quies is a judgement between Gladstone, undoubtedly the
> greatest Prime Minister of the nineteenth century, and
> Churchill, undoubtedly the greatest of the twentieth century.
> When I started writing this book I thought that Gladstone
> was, by a narrow margin, the greater man, certainly the more
> remarkable specimen of humanity. In the course of writing it
> I have changed my mind. I now put Churchill, with all his
> idiosyncrasies, his indulgences, his occasional childishness,
> but also his genius, his tenacity and his persistent ability, right
> or wrong, successful or unsuccessful, to be larger than life, as
> the greatest human being ever to occupy 10 Downing Street.

Greatness is difficult to measure. It tends to dissipate. With Churchill it took a long time to do so, and he would go on to serve another term as prime minister after 1951. The king, however, had less time left in his reign. The war had exhausted his already frail health. In September, Churchill told his own doctor that he was "shocked by the King's appearance." Moran reassured him that the king's doctors would limit his suffering. "That is all very well with an ordinary patient," Churchill replied, "but it does not apply to the Monarch. Under the Constitution, the duty of the king's doctors is to prolong his life as long as possible."

On September 23, Churchill "did a thing this morning that I haven't done in many years—I went down on my knees by my bedside & prayed."

The king lingered for a few more months. At dinner on February 5 he "was relaxed and contented. He retired to his room at 10.30 and was occupied with his personal affairs until about midnight when a watchman in the garden observed him affixing the latch of his bedroom window.... Then he went to bed and fell peacefully asleep."

By the following morning he was dead.

Churchill's private secretary found him "in bed, with papers scattered all over the blankets, a chewed cigar in his mouth. He said, 'I've got bad news, Prime Minister. The King died last night. I know nothing else.' 'Bad news? The worst,' said Churchill.... He threw aside all the papers on his bed, exclaiming, 'How unimportant these matters are.'" He was later seen "sitting up with tears in his eyes, staring straight ahead." "Seeking to reassure him, [Colville] said that he would find the new Queen charming, attractive, intelligent and immensely conscientious."

"I hardly know her, and she is only a child."

Churchill was called to broadcast the news. Often before making broadcasts he would joke about having another brandy or some-such. Not now. "What is the time?" he demanded. "We must hurry."

He had worked all day on his remarks but broke down while reading them. After delivering the broadcast, he shut himself inside the Cabinet Room. At the funeral, he attached a small card in his own handwriting to the wreath: "For Valour."

Churchill remained in office until April 1955. He went to see the Cabinet Room a final time. "The room was in darkness," Moran observed. "When the light was switched on it appeared in disarray, ready for the cleaners, the chairs, shrouded in their covers, pushed to one side, the ink-pots gone. Winston looked for a moment in bewilderment on the scene, then he turned on his heel and stumbled out into the hall."

Nearly a decade later, on January 24, 1965, he died. From the train on his final journey to be buried by his parents in Bladon churchyard, there were seen

two single figures . . . first on the flat roof of a small house a man standing at attention in his old R.A.F. uniform, saluting; and then in a field, some hundreds of yards away from the track, a simple farmer stopping work and standing, head bowed, and cap in hand.

ACKNOWLEDGMENTS

Alexander Hoyt put the idea for this book in my head and helped me overcome the qualms of a mildly republican heart. Wendy Wolf and Hugh Van Dusen have been stalwart. Margaret Riggs, Jeanette Gingold, and Sharon Gonzalez were models of diligence. The archivists at the Churchill Archives Centre, Windsor Castle, the University of York, and King's College London, and the librarians at the Boston Athenaeum, Harvard's Lamont and Widener libraries, and the Bilkent University library assisted me in numerous ways. Peter Hopkirk, Ezel Kural Shaw, and the late Stanford Shaw donated collections to Bilkent without which this book would have been much harder to write. Timothy Dickinson educated me in the nuances of monarchy. J. K. Rowling delivered a commencement address on the subject of failure that I shall not forget. Ian Klaus debated the distinctions between partnerships and alliances with me. Andrew Roberts took the time to review the manuscript.

I am grateful to every one of them.

Portions of the king's diaries not quoted from published sources are reproduced by permission of Her Majesty Queen Elizabeth II;

excerpts from the Alanbrooke, Dill, and Ismay papers by permission of the Trustees of the Liddell Hart Centre for Military Archives, King's College London; the diaries of Lord Halifax by permission of the Borthwick Institute, University of York; and excerpts from Churchill's published writings by permission of Curtis Brown, London, on behalf of the Estate of Sir Winston Churchill.

NOTES

All quotations come from the works that appear in the bibliography. Sources of quotations not attributed to a speaker directly in the text are identified below. Spellings appear as they are in the original.

CHAPTER ONE

1 *fascinated, browbeaten, cajoled* Spears, *Assignment to Catastrophe*, vol. 1, 104.

1 *boundless confidence* Wheeler-Bennett, *King George VI*, 328.

1 *Resign—Resign* Rhodes James, ed., "*Chips*," 247.

2 *curled like a question mark* Roberts, *The Holy Fox*, 230.

2 *could see at least three facets* Watt, *How War Came*, 79.

2 *high priest of the Respectable Tendency* Roberts, *Eminent Churchillians*, 16.

2 *a slight lisp* Roberts, *The Holy Fox*, 6.

2 *insinuating, but unlovable* Rhodes James, ed., "*Chips*," 256.

2 *uncomfortable bed fellow* Jenkins, *Churchill*, 416.

2 *far closer to him* Roberts, *The Holy Fox*, 201.

3 *demeanour was cool* Churchill, *The Second World War*, vol. 1, 523.

4 *It would be difficult to say yes* Colville, *The Fringes of Power*, 123.

4 *Winston was obdurate* Moran, *Winston Churchill*, 323.

7 *this strangely assorted pair* Thompson, *The Yankee Marlborough,* 140.

8 *as a set-piece contest* Roberts, *The Holy Fox,* 1.

9 *In times of danger* Kiernan, *Churchill,* 10.

CHAPTER TWO

11 *[i]t was not a tactful day* Wheeler-Bennett, *King George VI,* 4.

11 *on a note of apology* Ibid.

12 *Faithful but unfortunate* Cannadine, *In Churchill's Shadow,* 51.

12 *all Churchills were undoubtedly eccentric* Lees-Milne, *Ancestral Voices,* 50.

12 *Yankee mongrel* Colville, *The Churchillians,* 85.

14 *He is not loved, he is not feared* Brooks, *Devil's Decade,* 26–27.

16 *pale little ghost* Thompson, *The Yankee Marlborough,* 27–28.

17 *rather inky small boy* Rowse, *The Later Churchills,* 341.

17 *as wise as he was shrewd* Ibid., 297.

17 *The House of Hanover* Nicolson, *Diaries,* 407.

18 *gnashes* Shawcross, *Queen Elizabeth,* 466.

18 *bad starter* Wheeler-Bennett, *King George VI,* 33; Duff, *George and Elizabeth,* 39.

20 *grit and 'never say I'm beaten' spirit* Wheeler-Bennett, *King George VI,* 41.

CHAPTER THREE

24 *Medal-hunter* Churchill, *My Early Life,* 174; Thompson, *The Yankee Marlborough,* 87.

24 *You've heard of Winston Churchill* Rowse, *The Later Churchills,* 365.

25 *What the hell are you doing* Moffatt, *King George Was My Shipmate,* 18.

26 *distinctly startled* Wheeler-Bennett, *King George VI,* 95.

26 *Young Bertie had:* Moffatt, *King George Was My Shipmate,* 27.

26 *many a pearl* Kiernan, *Churchill,* 53.

28 *reluctance which inhibits Liberals* Bonham Carter, *Winston Churchill as I Knew Him,* 205.

28 *Blenheim rat* Brooks, *Devil's Decade,* 198.

28 *you could rat but you couldn't re-rat* Colville, *The Fringes of Power*, 345.

31 *what precisely was it ready for* Best, *Churchill and War*, 45.

32 *a floating kidney* Thompson, *The Yankee Marlborough*, 201, 209.

34 *mutual telegram* Duff, *George and Elizabeth*, 82.

CHAPTER FOUR

38 *a nice, quiet, well-bred mouse* Rhodes James, ed., *"Chips,"* 23.

38 *absolute slave* Ibid., 60.

38 *The Battle for the Throne* Ibid., 86.

38 *a party of lunatics* Lees-Milne, *Prophesying Peace*, 24.

39 *chatty, handy type of monarch* Hart-Davis, ed., *King's Counsellor*, 82.

40 *Nothing is here for tears* Bonham Carter, *Winston Churchill as I Knew Him*, 279.

40 *the cabin-boy made captain* Rowse, *The Later Churchills*, 447.

40 *half Machiavelli, half Milton* Rhodes James, ed., *"Chips,"* 143.

40 *Let this thing be settled. . . . We are all in false positions* Nicolson, *Diaries*, 170.

41 *unrelieved gloom* Wheeler-Bennett, *King George VI*, 276.

41 *shop-soiled American* Hart-Davis, ed., *King's Counsellor*, 414.

44 *Out of Office* Brooks, *Devil's Decade*, 197–98.

45 *an Ishmael in public life* Rhodes James, *Churchill*, 184.

45 *discovered that he was* Shawcross, *Queen Elizabeth*, 450.

CHAPTER FIVE

47 *It came in like a ravening wolf* Brooks, *Devil's Decade*, 13.

47 Tories who were ashamed: Kiernan, *Churchill*, 74.

47 *like the chamomile* Rhodes James, *Churchill*, 186.

48 *drowning man to a spar* Thompson, *The Yankee Marlborough*, 264.

49 *dual policy* Nicolson, *Marginal Comment*, 152.

50 *avenging march* Rowse, *The Later Churchills*, 445.

51 *Injudicious they may have been* Watt, *How War Came*, 77.

52 *You know, I am a trifle uneasy* Nicolson, *Marginal Comment*, 120.

52 *royally displeased* Wheeler-Bennett, *King George VI*, 335.

53 *as familiar as the voice* Pawle, *The War and Colonel Warden*, 56.

54 *Mush, Slush and Gush* Rhodes James, *Churchill*, 228.

54 *one ex-Serviceman* Wheeler-Bennett, *King George VI*, 348.

55 *was not bluffing* Ibid., 349.

55 *You might think* Colville, *The Fringes of Power*, 590.

56 *waving his whisky-and-soda* Nicolson, *Diaries*, 212–13.

59 *An elderly gentleman* Roberts, *The Holy Fox*, 179.

CHAPTER SIX

63 *faithful chela* Roberts, *Eminent Churchillians*, 41.

64 *hard to be Kaiser*, Steinberg, *Bismarck*, 3.

65 *he venerated tradition* Ismay, *Memoirs*, 270.

65 *Dukes tended to believe* Ziegler, "Churchill and the Monarchy," in Blake and Louis, eds., *Churchill*, 187.

66 *semi-Royal* Pawle, *The War and Colonel Warden*, 75.

66 *elephantine shuffle* Young, ed., *The Diaries of Sir Robert Bruce Lockhart*, vol. 2, 327.

68 *hurly-burly* Churchill, *Great Contemporaries*, 149.

69 *moderate and politically uninterested* Roberts, *Eminent Churchillians*, 8.

69 *temperance, magnificence* Nicolson, *Marginal Comment*, 8.

69 *despairer* Moran, *Winston Churchill*, 745.

70 *a very good combination* Roberts, *The Holy Fox*, 270.

70 *adored funny operations* Roberts, *Eminent Churchillians*, 63.

71 *If he were a woman* Thompson, *The Yankee Marlborough*, 37.

71 *Dilly Dally* Alanbrooke, *War Diaries*, xl.

71 *killed men* Johnson, *Churchill*, 114.

72 *would often relapse* Pawle, *The War and Colonel Warden*, 145.

72 *a great aristocrat* Wheeler-Bennett, *King George VI*, 519.

72 *What shall I say* Hart-Davis, ed., *King's Counsellor*, 37.

73 *the luckiest general* Young, ed., *The Diaries of Sir Robert Bruce Lockhart*, vol. 2, 243.

73 *still waters running deep* Astley, *The Inner Circle*, 34.

73 *Characteristic of straightforward* Ibid., 70.

75 *thought fast* Fraser, *Alanbrooke*, 122.

77 *Whatever the P.M.'s shortcomings* Colville, *The Fringes of Power*, 489.

77 *apostle of the offensive* Kiernan, *Churchill,* 142–43.

78 *Brooke was the only man* Colville, *The Churchillians,* 143.

79 a cavalryman out of his depth: Richard Ollard, "Churchill and the Navy," in Blake and Louis, eds., *Churchill,* 394.

80 Churchill was said to be afraid: Young, ed., *The Diaries of Sir Robert Bruce Lockhart,* vol. 2, 352.

80 *good at trying* Lees-Milne, *Ancestral Voices,* 130–31.

82 *This greatly amused Churchill* Pawle, *The War and Colonel Warden,* 108.

83 *in the way Lloyd George was* Lees-Milne, *Prophesying Peace,* 88.

83 *he has genius* Brooks, *Devil's Decade,* 196.

84 *sidles away from one* Rhodes James, ed., "*Chips,*" 232–33.

84 *he seems to contract* Ibid., 269.

84 *tilt at windmills* Thompson, *The Yankee Marlborough,* 37.

85 *till it shone* Jenkins, *Churchill,* 510.

85 *picnics* Shawcross, *Queen Elizabeth,* 514, 568.

86 *small drop of arsenic* Roberts, *Eminent Churchillians,* 9.

86 *selective listener* Pawle, *The War and Colonel Warden,* 204.

86 *He wanted no other reward* Moran, *Winston Churchill,* 259.

CHAPTER SEVEN

90 *I went to the ironmonger's* Astley, *The Inner Circle,* 205.

90 *so adjacent* Brooks, *Devil's Decade,* 195.

92 *Lift* Hastings, *Finest Years,* 439.

94 *heart attack* Moran, *Winston Churchill,* 614.

95 *He felt ill* Young, ed., *The Diaries of Sir Robert Bruce Lockhart,* vol. 2, 483.

96 *a cross between comic opera* Colville in Wheeler-Bennett, ed., *Action This Day,* 71.

98 *It was Churchill's greatest deficiency* Rhodes James, *Churchill,* 349.

101 *sipper not a guzzler* Jenkins, *Churchill,* 356.

101 *Cat, darling* Colville, *The Fringes of Power,* 172.

103 *with his schoolboy's grin* Hart-Davis, ed., *King's Counsellor,* 344n1.

103 *tendency to morbidness* Wheeler-Bennett, *King George VI,* 155.

104 *demon driver* Ibid., 109.

104 *fling himself* Pawle, *The War and Colonel Warden*, 150.

104 *hippopotamus* Gilbert, *Winston S. Churchill*, vol. 7, 37.

CHAPTER EIGHT

107 *underwent the most dramatic reversal* Roberts, *Eminent Churchillians*, 1.

107 *He rushed up the steps* Gilbert, *Winston S. Churchill*, vol. 6, 4.

108 *could be read both ways* Best, *Churchill and War*, 107.

109 *Winston problem* Colville, *The Fringes of Power*, 111.

109 *Deputy Prime Minister* Ibid.

110 *staring into space* Bradford, *The Reluctant King*, 375.

112 *mad plans* Alanbrooke, *War Diaries*, 187.

114 six divisions: Lees-Milne, *Ancestral Voices*, 97.

114 *frog speech* Colville, *The Fringes of Power*, 272; See also Douglas Johnson, "Churchill and France," in Blake and Louis, eds., *Churchill*, 44–45.

118 *two tongues* Gilbert, *Winston S. Churchill*, vol. 7, 357.

119 *was standing* Hastings, *Finest Years*, 18.

120 *measured in rubies* Colville, *The Fringes of Power*, 223.

120 *George, why* Lees-Milne, *Prophesying Peace*, 70.

121 *Whither thou goest* Moran, *Winston Churchill*, 6.

122 *the greatest worshippers* Wheeler-Bennett, *King George VI*, 254.

122 *weeping, and crying* Ibid., 380.

125 *just like a small boy* Alanbrooke, *War Diaries*, 139.

126 *triphibious* Gilbert, *Winston S. Churchill*, vol. 7, 467.

126 *great amphibian* Thompson, *The Yankee Marlborough*, 327.

128 *What was that noise* Rhodes James, ed., *"Chips,"* 279.

128 *Go to Hell, man* Colville, *The Fringes of Power*, 278.

128 *My time will come* Pawle, *The War and Colonel Warden*, 82.

128 *Pugnacious old bugger* Ibid., 70.

128 *There goes the bloody British Empire* Colville, *The Fringes of Power*, 341.

128 *Good old Winnie*, Ismay, *Memoirs*, 183–84.

129 *Oh, ain't she lovely* Wheeler-Bennett, *King George VI*, 467.

130 *the unmistakable whirr-whirr* Shawcross, *Queen Elizabeth*, 522–23.

131 *immense catacomb* Hart-Davis, ed., *King's Counsellor*, 63.

131 *valuable small Dutch landscapes* Shawcross, *Queen Elizabeth*, 517.

CHAPTER NINE

135 *slow-time* Pawle, *The War and Colonel Warden,* 177.

137 *Ah yes, Mr. Prime Minister* Young, ed., *The Diaries of Sir Robert Bruce Lockhart,* vol. 2, 107.

139 They dined on smoked salmon: Details from menus in the President's Office Files.

139 *very blun[t]* Wheeler-Bennett, *King George VI,* 529.

140 *Suddenly there was a pause* Pawle, *The War and Colonel Warden,* 6–7.

140 *Good God* Gilbert, *Winston S. Churchill* vol. 6, 1268.

142 *from Casablanca* Thompson, *The Yankee Marlborough,* 329, 339.

142 *poor little English donkey* Colville in Wheeler-Bennett, ed., *Action This Day,* 96 n1.

147 *resulted in good argument* Alanbrooke, *War Diaries,* 249.

151 *One young officer* Hart-Davis, ed., *King's Counsellor,* 80.

153 *the world of Walt Disney* Pawle, *The War and Colonel Warden,* 189.

153 *We must mind our Ps and Qs* Broad, *The War That Churchill Waged,* 238.

156 *rugs and carpets and curtains* Wheeler-Bennett, *King George VI,* 569, 570n, 576, 578.

158 *The guests sat transfixed* Ismay, *Memoirs,* 341; Astley, *The Inner Circle,* 124.

158 *appalled by his own impotence* Moran, *Winston Churchill,* 141.

CHAPTER TEN

162 *kept dodging out* Gilbert, *Winston S. Churchill,* vol. 7, 709.

163 *supreme climax...the keystone of the arch* Broad, *The War That Churchill Waged,* 281.

163 *Slim Jan* Colville, *The Churchillians,* 134.

163 *surrogate uncle* Roberts, *Masters and Commanders,* photo insert, n.p.

163 *mind moved majestically* Churchill, *The Second World War,* vol. 4, 386.

163 *Smuts is not happy* Wheeler-Bennett, *King George VI,* 594.

164 *old Smuts* Hart Davis, ed., *King's Counsellor,* 172.

164 *be secured at all costs* Wheeler-Bennett, *King George VI,* 596.

169 *sixth hour of the sixth day* Young, ed., *The Diaries of Sir Robert Bruce Lockhart*, vol. 2, 319.

170 *had a jolly day* Churchill, *The Second World War*, vol. 6, 13.

170 *he would have been happier still* Ismay, *Memoirs*, 358.

171 *on the top of the Victoria Tower* Lees-Milne, *Prophesying Peace*, 90.

171 *Come in* Gilbert, *Winston Churchill*, vol. 7, 1057.

172 *gold fish in a stone pool* Astley, *The Inner Circle*, 183.

172 *fiercely controversial* Broad, *The War That Churchill Waged*, 345.

172 *black with Fortresses* Colville, *The Fringes of Power*, 588.

173 *felt the strain* Shawcross, *Queen Elizabeth*, 591.

174 *orderly and good humoured* Lees-Milne, *Prophesying Peace*, 187–88.

176 *files, papers, pieces of broken furniture* Astley, *The Inner Circle*, 218–19.

176 *He did not seem greatly interested* Moran, *Winston Churchill*, 270.

DENOUEMENT

177 *Five million against us* Pawle, *The War and Colonel Warden*, 401.

177 *Keep alert* Ibid., 402.

182 *relaxed and contented* Wheeler-Bennett, *King George VI*, 803.

182 *The worst* Shawcross, *Queen Elizabeth*, 653.

183 *two single figures* Leslie Rowan in Wheeler-Bennett, ed., *Action This Day*, 265.

BIBLIOGRAPHY

Alanbrooke Papers, Liddell Hart Centre for Military Archives, King's College London.

Winston Churchill Papers, Churchill Archives Centre, Cambridge University.

Dill Papers, Liddell Hart Centre for Military Archives, King's College London.

Halifax Papers, Borthwick Institute for Archives, University of York.

Ismay Papers, Liddell Hart Centre for Military Archives, King's College London.

President's Office Files, Franklin D. Roosevelt Presidential Library, Hyde Park.

Royal Archives, King George VI Diaries (RA GVI/PRIV/DIARY).

Astley, Joan Bright. *The Inner Circle: A View of War at the Top.* London: Hutchinson, 1971.

Berlin, Isaiah. *Personal Impressions.* Princeton, NJ: Princeton University Press, 2001 (1949).

Best, Geoffrey. *Churchill and War.* London: Hambledon & London, 2005.

Blake, Robert, and William Roger Louis, eds. *Churchill.* Oxford: Oxford University Press, 1993.

Bonham Carter, Violet. *Winston Churchill as I Knew Him.* London: Pan Books, 1967 (1965).

Bradford, Sarah. *The Reluctant King: The Life and Reign of George VI, 1895–1952*. New York: St. Martin's Press, 1989.

British Broadcasting Corporation. Interviews with John Martin (11 Nov. 1973), Robert Boothby (24 Nov. 1970), Nancy Astor (23 Nov. 1977), at www.bbc.co.uk.

Broad, Lewis. *The War That Churchill Waged*. London: Hutchinson, 1960.

Brooks, Collin. *Devil's Decade: Portraits of the Nineteen-Thirties*. London: Macdonald, 1948.

Cannadine, David. *In Churchill's Shadow: Confronting the Past in Modern Britain*. Oxford: Oxford University Press, 2003.

Churchill, Winston S. *Great Contemporaries*. New York: W. W. Norton, 1991 (1930).

———. *My Early Life: A Roving Commission*. London: Reprint Society, 1944 (1930).

———. *Painting as a Pastime*. London: Odhams Press, 1949 (1948).

———. *The Second World War* (6 vols.). London: Cassell, 1948–54.

Colville, John. *The Churchillians*. London: Weidenfeld & Nicolson, 1981.

———. *The Fringes of Power: Downing Street Diaries, 1939–1955*. London: Hodder and Stoughton, 1985.

Danchev, Alex, and Daniel Todman, eds. *Alanbrooke, Field Marshal Lord, War Diaries 1939–1945*. London: Phoenix Press, 2002 (2001).

Duff, David. *George and Elizabeth: A Royal Marriage*. London: Collins, 1983.

Eden, Anthony. *Facing the Dictators*. Boston: Houghton Mifflin, 1962.

Fraser, David. *Alanbrooke*. London: Hamlyn Paperbacks, 1983 (1982).

Gilbert, Martin. *Winston S. Churchill* (8 vols., Nos. 1 and 2 with Randolph Churchill). London: Heinemann, 1966–82.

Hart-Davis, Duff, ed. *End of an Era: Letters and Journals of Sir Alan Lascelles from 1887 to 1920*. London: Hamish Hamilton, 1988 (1986).

———. *In Royal Service: The Letters and Journals of Sir Alan Lascelles*, vol. 2, *1920–1936*. London: Hamish Hamilton, 1989.

———. *King's Counsellor. Abdication and War: The Diaries of Sir Alan Lascelles*. London: Weidenfeld & Nicolson, 2006.

Hastings, Max. *Finest Years: Churchill as Warlord, 1940–45*. London: HarperPress, 2009.

Ismay, Hastings. *The Memoirs of General the Lord Ismay.* London: Heinemann, 1960.

Jenkins, Roy. *Churchill.* London: Pan Books, 2002 (2001).

Johnson, Paul. *Churchill.* New York: Penguin, 2010 (2009).

Kiernan, R. H. *Churchill.* London: George G. Harrap, 1942.

Lees-Milne, James. *Ancestral Voices.* London: Faber and Faber, 1984 (1975).

———. *Prophesying Peace.* London: Michael Russell, 2003 (1977).

Lukacs, John. *Remembered Past: John Lukacs on History, Historians and Historical Knowledge: A Reader.* Wilmington, DE: ISI Books, Intercollegiate Studies Institute, 2005.

MacNalty, Arthur Salusbury. *The Three Churchills.* London: Essential Books, 1949.

Moffatt, James. *King George Was My Shipmate.* London: Stanley Paul, 1940.

Moran, Charles McMoran Wilson. *Winston Churchill: The Struggle for Survival, 1940–1965.* London: Constable, 1966.

Newby, Eric. *Love and War in the Apennines.* London: Picador, 1983 (1971).

Nicolson, Harold. *Diaries and Letters, 1907–1964,* ed. Nigel Nicolson. London: Phoenix, 2005 (2004).

———. *Marginal Comment, January 6–August 4, 1939.* London: Constable, 1939.

Norwich, John Julius, ed. *The Duff Cooper Diaries.* London: Phoenix, 2006 (2005).

Pawle, Gerald. With a foreword by W. Averell Harriman. *The War and Colonel Warden.* London: George G. Harrap, 1963.

Payn, Graham, and Sheridan Morley, eds. *The Noël Coward Diaries.* Boston: Little Brown, 1982.

Rhodes James, Robert, ed. *"Chips": The Diaries of Sir Henry Channon.* London: Weidenfeld & Nicolson, 1993 (1967).

———. *Churchill: A Study in Failure, 1900–1939.* London: Weidenfeld & Nicolson, 1990 (1970).

———. *A Spirit Undaunted: The Political Role of George VI.* London: Abacus, 1999 (1998).

Roberts, Andrew. *Eminent Churchillians*. New York: Simon & Schuster, 1994.

———. *The Holy Fox: The Life of Lord Halifax*. London: Phoenix Giant, 1997 (1991).

———. *Masters and Commanders: How Four Titans Won the War in the West, 1941–1945*. New York: HarperCollins, 2009.

Rose, Kenneth. *King George V*. London: Weidenfeld & Nicolson, 1983.

———. *Kings, Queens and Courtiers: Intimate Portraits of the Royal House of Windsor from Its Foundation to the Present Day*. London: Weidenfeld & Nicolson, 1985.

Rowse, A. L. *The Later Churchills*. London: Penguin Books, 1971 (1958).

Salter, Arthur. *Personality in Politics: Studies of Contemporary Statesmen*. London: Faber and Faber, 1947.

Seaman, Mark. *Bravest of the Brave*. London: Michael O'Mara Books, 1999.

Shawcross, William. *Queen Elizabeth: The Queen Mother*. London: Pan Books, 2010 (2009).

Spears, Edward. *Assignment to Catastrophe*, 2 vols. London: William Heinemann, 1954.

Steinberg, Jonathan. *Bismarck: A Life*. Oxford: Oxford University Press, 2011.

Steiner, Zara. *The Triumph of the Dark: European International History, 1933–1939*. Oxford: Oxford University Press, 2011.

Taylor, A. J. P., Robert Rhodes James, J. H. Plumb, Basil Liddell Hart, and Anthony Storr. *Churchill: Four Faces and the Man*. Harmondsworth, London: Penguin, 1973 (1969).

Taylor, S. J. *The Great Outsiders: Northcliffe, Rothermere and the Daily Mail*. London: Weidenfeld & Nicolson, 1996.

Thompson, R. W. *The Yankee Marlborough*. London: George Allen & Unwin, 1963.

Trevor-Roper, Hugh. *The Wartime Journals*, ed. Richard Davenport-Hines. London: I. B. Taurus, 2012.

Watt, Donald Cameron. *How War Came: The Immediate Origins of the Second World War, 1938–1939*. New York: Pantheon Books, 1989.

Weinberg, Gerhard. "Some Myths of World War II," *The Journal of Military History* 75 (July 2011), pp. 701–18.

Wheeler-Bennett, John, ed. *Action This Day.* London: Macmillan, 1968.

——. *King George VI: His Life and Reign.* London: Macmillan, 1958.

Young, Kenneth, ed. *The Diaries of Sir Robert Bruce Lockhart,* 2 vols. London: Macmillan, 1980.

INDEX